HERE'S WHAT PEOPLE ARE SAYING ABOUT KATIE J. TRENT AND *RECIPES FOR A SWEET CHILD*...

Is your child struggling with anger, anxiety, or jealousy? Are you concerned about laziness, gossiping, or peer pressure? Katie Trent has addressed these issues and many more in her new book, *Recipes for a Sweet Child*. The wisdom and practical suggestions she offers are geared toward helping moms and dads nurture a robust faith in their kids and strengthen the key relationships in their children's lives.

—*Jim Daly*
President, Focus on the Family

Recipes for a Sweet Child is incredibly practical, helpful, and transformative for the whole family! I absolutely love reading the devotional to prepare my own heart and then engaging my kids to participate in fun activities and in-depth conversation questions. This is the perfect way to start our homeschool day! This resource has led to wonderful conversations and Holy Spirit epiphanies about anger, sadness, fear, jealousy, sibling rivalry, and so much more. Katie uses her experience as a licensed clinical social worker to give incredible tools for helping kids with their big emotions and helping parents know how to respond in a loving but effective way. Whether you are a parent, grandparent, or kids' ministry leader, this book will have a profound impact on the kids in your life and on your own heart! It will also connect you deeply as you engage in the memory-making activities together. This is my new go-to homeschooling book, and I know I will use it over and over again with my kids.

—*Sarah Holmstrom*
Coauthor, *Raising Prayerful Kids*

What a delightful and delicious resource to feed the family and soul! I always say, if you can't make it fun, make it edible. But Katie has made it both fun and edible, while helping young kids to grow emotionally and spiritually. Though my boys are older now and "too cool" for some of the activities, I know I can extract some great discussion prompts and recipes to share with them while studying God's Word.

—*Jennifer Cabrera*
Hifalutin Homeschooler
Author, speaker, and homeschool mom

Wow! What an amazing, powerful, practical, and deeply insightful book. This is literally a handbook for those who are beginning the great adventure of homeschool. Katie shows her rich wisdom from her own journey and experience. This book is an answer to the prayer of so many who face the challenges and hurdles of being a homeschool mom. No matter what hurdle you're presented to face or may encounter in the future in homeschool, Katie has diligently created a blueprint for success!

—*Dr. Michael Maiden*
Senior pastor, Church for the Nations, Phoenix, AZ

Katie serves up a real treat with *Recipes for a Sweet Child*. She makes it easy for busy homeschool moms to teach vital social and emotional skills with these unique devotions. You'll find encouragement for your quiet time and practical ideas for family fun time. You'll not only make delicious desserts with the related recipes, but you'll also make precious memories together.

—*Melanie Wilson, Ph.D.*
Clinical psychologist; host, *The Homeschool Sanity Show*

I'm all about having fun as a family, and Katie J. Trent has hit the nail on the head with her book *Recipes for a Sweet Child*. She combines fun activities with concepts your child needs to learn. From anger and fear to tattling, whining, and lying to relationship issues, Katie offers practical, biblical activities to help your child work through these issues. Not only does she give you biblical solutions, she has fun cooking activities for each emotion. I don't know about you, but my kids always paid more attention when they saw food involved in our family time. I wish this resource was available when my kids were at home, but I'm thankful I can use it with my grandkids.

—*Kerry Beck*
Author, *How to Homeschool My Child*
and *Raising Leaders, Not Followers*

36 Baking Devotions for the Whole Family

RECIPES
for a
SWEET CHILD

Creative, Bible-Based Activities to
Help Your Family Thrive

Author of *Dishing Up Devotions*
KATIE J. TRENT

RECIPES FOR A SWEET CHILD
Creative, Bible-Based Activities to Help Your Family Thrive

katiejtrent.com

ISBN: 979-8-88769-000-1
eBook ISBN: 979-8-88769-001-8
Printed in Colombia
© 2023 by Katie J. Trent

Whitaker House
1030 Hunt Valley Circle
New Kensington, PA 15068
www.whitakerhouse.com

Library of Congress Control Number: 2023934611

1 2 3 4 5 6 7 8 9 10 11 ⨃ 30 29 28 27 26 25 24 '23

DEDICATION

To all the mamas out there doing their best to love and teach their kiddos: you're building a legacy that future generations will thank you for. Keep going! I'm praying for you and want you to know that you're never alone. *You can do this!*

CONTENTS

*Gluten-free; most recipes offer conventional options

Section Three: Relational Challenges

*Gluten-free; most recipes offer conventional options

*Gluten-free; most recipes offer conventional options

ACKNOWLEDGEMENTS

I am so grateful to all of the incredible people who helped make this book possible. I'm honored to work again with the phenomenal team at Whitaker House, whose dedication to excellence and equipping the body of Christ shines in everything they do. Thank you, Christine Whitaker, for believing in me and this project. Thank you, Peg Fallon, for being so good at your job and helping to polish my words and fix my mistakes. Thank you to Becky Speer for your creativity and design expertise. And a special thank you to Cheryl Ricker, my agent and friend. I'm so glad we get to take this journey together. Your prayers and support have encouraged me every step of the way. I love working with you!

I'm also thankful for my unbelievably supportive husband James, without whom I couldn't do what I do. Your sacrifices for me and our family humble me daily. I love and appreciate our children, Kendra and Jordan, who allow me to share such personal details about their lives in order to help other families around the world. You're the reason I do what I do. I'm so proud to be your mother.

I thank Jesus for the blessing of being able to do something I love and giving me the words to write to equip and encourage others along their journeys as well.

And I want to thank everyone who helped launch my first book and cheered me on along the way with this one. Your support means so much to me! Thanks for your prayers, encouragement, and helping me spread the word about *Dishing Up Devotions*. Special thanks to my team of *baking buddies* who tested recipes and offered feedback. I appreciate each of you: Molly Cash, Jenn Velchez, Stephanie LeBlanc, and Mandy Mae Johnson.

INTRODUCTION:
HOW TO USE THIS BOOK

Hi, sweet friend. I'm so glad you're here! I know how daunting this journey of motherhood can be. That's why I wrote this book—for you and for me, so we can feel confident navigating those daily challenges that pop up at the most inconvenient times.

You can go through the book chapter by chapter as a preventative teaching tool or skip right to the issue you're facing. Also, there's no right or wrong way to utilize the various features in each chapter. While I recommend beginning with the devotion and prayer (for your own sanity and peace of mind), you can choose which activities to utilize in the way that works best for your family. They can be done in a single day, spread throughout the week, or spaced out even longer if you wish. They're simply tools to help you feel confident and capable as you teach and disciple your kiddos.

Each chapter begins with a devotion to encourage and equip you regarding a struggle you may experience with your child. You'll also find a guided prayer at the end of each devotion.

The next section is what I call the *teachable moment*. This is a quick and easy lesson with a biblical focus to help you address the emotional, behavioral, or relational issue with your child(ren). I try to give ideas for various age groups, but feel free to adapt them to meet your family's unique needs.

You can utilize the discussion guide or *conversation connection* either with the teachable moment or at a separate time. It will help you dive deeper and explore the root causes of the struggle with your kids as you assist them in making connections between their actions, their faith, and the impact their choices have on themselves and others.

The *family fun* section includes a fun game or activity for you to do as a family to reinforce the teaching while also building a heart-to-heart connection with your kids. Lessons stick when we make beautiful memories together. We all struggle with different issues, but by connecting and having fun together, we cultivate healthier relationships and open the lines of communication. It's especially important for us as parents to ensure our children feel loved and secure as we build a biblical foundation and teach life skills. Have fun and enjoy these moments together.

Finally, you'll notice the *baking buddies* and *recipe* at the end of each chapter. The *baking buddies* section provides you with a little script or introduction to the recipe to help make the connection between it and the challenge you're addressing that week. They also include a Scripture related to that week's theme.

I included a variety of recipes for those with allergies and dietary restrictions, but feel free to adapt the recipes to work for your family. They're simply another tool for connection and conversation. Many of these recipes can be made gluten-free. You may also want to share these goodies with friends, relatives, neighbors, coworkers, and church members. A little hospitality can go a long way in spreading the love of Christ to those around us!

A Final Note

For the Scripture references, feel free to use whichever Bible works best for your child or your family. You can search for the stories in various children's Bibles, read them directly from your family Bible, or do both. You'll notice I reference a variety of translations and note which one I've used next to the Scripture. If there's no notation, it's from the *Holy Bible, New Living Translation*, which is an easy one for younger kids to understand. You can always read the Scriptures from the Bible you prefer rather than the one I've cited.

Additionally, you will find tons of resources and Bible stories online if your child does better watching short clips. However, you should watch first to make sure it's what you're seeking. The most important thing is that we're introducing our children to the Bible and helping them learn how to apply God's Word to their everyday lives. We want to demonstrate that the Bible has a solution for every problem we face. Hebrews 4:12 teaches us, *"For the word of God is alive and powerful. It is sharper than the sharpest two-edged sword, cutting between soul and spirit, between joint and marrow. It exposes our innermost thoughts and desires."*

We're planting seeds that we will continue to nurture as our children grow, so don't be afraid to meet them right where they're at today. Pray. And trust God is working in and through you as you train up your children.

I pray this resource equips and encourages you as you endeavor to build your family's faith and grow in relationship with one another.

Have fun, do your best, and trust God with the rest.

Blessings,
Katie

SECTION ONE

EMOTIONAL CHALLENGES

1

ANGER

*And "don't sin by letting anger control you." Don't let the sun go
down while you are still angry.*
—Ephesians 4:26

"That's it! I can't take it anymore! Go to your room!"

Even as an adult, I still find myself losing my temper. It builds and
builds until I finally explode and end up yelling at my kids, despite the fact
that I know better. The worst part is when I hear my kids repeat some of
the phrases that came out of my own angry mouth. Yikes!

In the daily grind of life and parenting, it's impossible to avoid feelings
of anger. The good news is, God doesn't expect us to never feel this emotion. It can be normal and healthy. However, the Bible clearly states that we
can't let angry feelings lead to angry and sinful actions and words.

Counselors call anger a secondary emotion. This means it's usually an
indicator of a deeper issue. It may be masking other feelings like betrayal,
rejection, embarrassment, or fear. When anger rears its ugly head, it's best
to get to the root of the problem instead of simply trying to squash the
anger itself.

When my kids are angry, we first take time to calm down. Whether it's time alone in their room, holding them, or helping them through deep-breathing exercises, we focus on getting a handle on the anger before we discuss or address the issue. Once everyone is calm, we can then explore thoughts and feelings that triggered the anger.

For children who are external or verbal processors, talking it out is most helpful. Those who need time to process internally might require time alone to reflect or write down their thoughts. In either case, they will grow the most when they examine the thoughts they experienced before they blew up and label the deeper feelings that triggered the anger. You can then work with your kids on coping skills.

In our household, we regularly practice deep-breathing exercises—breathing deeply in through the nose and slowly exhaling through the mouth—along with the art of taking a time-out to calm down before we communicate. From the time our kids were little, we frequently reminded them, "It's okay to be mad, but it's not okay to be bad."

Parents' Prayer

God, please give me wisdom to help my children with their anger. Help me remain calm and communicate clearly with love. Reveal thoughts and feelings that trigger their anger outbursts and equip me with the tools to help them learn to control their emotions. In Jesus's name I pray. Amen.

Teachable Moment

Create a poster with as many descriptive feelings as you can think of. Appendix B provides a list of emotions to assist you. Discuss how anger often masks other emotions. Create and decorate angry masks and talk about why it's important to find out what's happening inside when we feel mad. Make a list of some of your kids' most common feelings masked by their anger, such as embarrassment, disappointment, fear, rejection, loneliness, etc.

Then, when your kids have displayed anger, ask them to consider what emotion their angry mask is really hiding. Pull out the mask or feeling list if they need help identifying their primary emotion. Practice completing this sentence once they're calm:

I feel _____ when _____ because _____. I want/need _____.

Our baking connection for this lesson relates to volcanoes, so you can also take this time to study and learn more about volcanoes together and discuss how volcanoes are safe as long as they are not exploding—just like our anger isn't a bad thing as long as we control it.

Conversation Connection

» Did you know it's easier to show anger than it is to share your heart? Why do you think that is?

» Name some feelings that anger might be hiding.

» What were you thinking or telling yourself before you got angry?

» How can you calm yourself down the next time you start to feel angry?

» How can I help you when you feel really mad? What do you need from me in those tough moments?

» What are some ways a person can end up sinning when they are angry?

» How can you keep yourself from sinning even when you feel upset?

Family Fun

Anger is like lava—when it spills out, it hurts everyone it touches. Play a game of Don't Touch the Lava. Shout, "The floor is lava!" and then everyone has five seconds to get both feet off the ground in whatever way they can. You can jump from pillows to blankets to furniture, or make it a learning game by placing different letters, words, geographical locations, or math facts around the room and having the kids hop from place to place until they land on the right one. Be sure to tape them down on hard floors so they don't slide around.

Baking Buddies

The Bible teaches us that *"A hot-tempered person starts fights; a cool-tempered person stops them"* (Proverbs 15:18). Have you ever seen a volcano? It's filled with hot magma. Pressure builds with gas bubbles until it eventually explodes onto the surface as lava.

The same thing happens to us when we allow our anger to build without dealing with it; eventually, we explode and hurt those around us. Today we're going to make Don't Blow it Lava Cakes to remind us not to explode when we feel angry.

DON'T BLOW IT LAVA CAKES

(GLUTEN-FREE)

Ingredients

8 oz. semisweet baking chocolate

1 cup unsalted butter

6 large eggs

4 large egg yolks

⅔ cup powdered sugar

½ cup gluten-free 1:1 baking flour

1 tsp. vanilla extract

½ tsp. salt

2 tbsp. softened butter to grease ramekins

2 tbsp. cocoa powder for dusting

4 ramekins (8 oz. baking dishes)

Directions

Preheat oven to 450°F.

Melt butter and chocolate in a double boiler over medium heat for about 3-5 minutes. If you don't have a double boiler, fill a small pot with 1-2 inches of water and turn the stove on medium so the water simmers. Place a heatproof bowl that fits snugly over the top (without touching the water) and put your ingredients in the bowl to melt from the steam.

Stir constantly, removing from heat when the chocolate is mostly melted.

In a medium bowl, whisk eggs and yolks until fluffy.

Sift the flour and powdered sugar together in a large bowl.

Add chocolate, eggs, vanilla, and salt to the flour mixture, whisking until smooth.

Butter and dust each ramekin with cocoa powder. Be sure to coat them well.

Pour batter into ramekins and then place ramekins on a cookie sheet.

Bake for 10-12 minutes, or until the tops have puffed up and the sides are firm. The centers should still be soft and jiggly.

Allow the ramekins to cool for 3-5 minutes. Then use the edge of a knife to gently loosen the cakes from the sides.

Use a small dessert plate and place it over top of the ramekin, then carefully flip the plate and ramekin over to release the cake.

Dust the top with powdered sugar or add a scoop of ice cream or whipped cream if desired. Serve warm.

Here's an alternative, easier recipe for one individual-sized dessert:

DON'T BLOW IT LAVA MUG CAKE
(GLUTEN-FREE)

Ingredients

¼ cup 1:1 gluten-free baking flour (or regular all-purpose flour)
¼ cup granulated sugar
2 tbsp. cocoa powder
Pinch of salt
3 tbsp. unsalted butter, melted
1 large egg
½ tsp. vanilla extract
2 tbsp. semisweet chocolate chips
1 tbsp. water

Directions

Use a microwave-safe mug. Add melted butter, milk, egg, and vanilla. Whisk to combine.

In a small bowl, whisk together flour, sugar, cocoa, baking powder, and salt with a fork until well-combined. Add to mug and stir until incorporated.

Place the chocolate chips in the center of the mug and drizzle the water over the top of the batter.

Microwave for 1-2 minutes, or until the cake rises to the top and the edges look set. The center will still be a little wet, shiny, and slightly sticky to the touch, but not raw. I recommend cooking for 1 minute, checking, then cooking for another 15-30 seconds at a time so you don't overcook it.

Allow to cool for about 5 minutes before eating.

1

SADNESS

*A cheerful heart brings a smile to your face; a sad heart makes it hard
to get through the day.*
—Proverbs 15:13 (MSG)

Our daughter went through a period of time when she frequently struggled with sadness. She spent a lot of time teary-eyed and talking about friends she missed and things that used to be. We had hours of conversations. It seemed like the more she dwelt on her sadness, the worse it became. Sadness can be addicting.

Something happens when we dive into feelings of sadness. I still recall a time during my teen years where I loved to feel sad. I would listen to sad country songs, watch sad movies, and just sit in the midst of those feelings of despair. Sadness pulls you in and drains the life from you. It truly does make it hard to get through the day.

We should acknowledge, validate, and normalize our children's feelings. However, we also want to make sure we're providing them with the tools they need to overcome their emotions. Feelings are indicators, but we mustn't allow them to become dictators. When we let our feelings take over, we will always end up in trouble.

We want to help our kids process their emotions. When counseling clients, I often share the idea that our feelings are like liquid filling a cup. If we don't deal with them, our feelings suddenly fill us to the brim. When that happens, we lose our ability to cope. A single drop added to an already full cup will always lead to overflow—and a big mess. So we need to regularly take time to empty our cups.

There are many ways to increase our capacity to cope with the everyday stressors we face and the overwhelming feelings they can create. Journaling can help our kids appropriately express their thoughts and feelings. Talking about what's bothering us makes a difference as well. Sometimes, we just need to do things that bring us joy. Sunshine, physical activity, a delicious treat, time with friends, or a favorite activity can all bring a smile to our faces and help us cope with any lingering sadness. It also benefits us to spend a few minutes in prayer, thanking God for the many blessings in our lives.

Parents' Prayer

Holy Spirit, thank You for being our comforter. I pray You would comfort my children as they experience sadness. Help them to experience the fullness of Your joy. Show me ways to equip them to better cope with the sadness. In Jesus's name I pray. Amen.

Teachable Moment

Where do feelings come from? Are they buried deep inside? Do our feelings come from the things that happen to and around us? Do we have any control over them? Did you know our feelings actually come from our thoughts? When we learn to pay attention to our thoughts and change them, we can change our feelings too.

Imagine two people stepping outside into the pouring rain. The first person thinks, *Oh great! I hate rain! It's going to ruin everything.* How do you think they would feel? (Sad, mad, disappointed, frustrated, etc.) Now imagine the second person thinks, *I love the rain! I can splash in puddles and my flowers are going to bloom!* How do you think they'd feel? (Happy, thankful, excited, etc.)

Both people experienced the same thing at the same time, so why did one of them feel happy while the other felt sad? Their thoughts about the situation created their feelings. So this week, we're going to focus on our thoughts and how they impact our feelings. Each time we feel sad, we're going to stop and think about what we're telling ourselves and how those thoughts are making us feel. Then together, we will come up with some different thoughts to change our feelings. (I recommend keeping a journal to track the thoughts, feelings, and behaviors when your child feels sad. Young kids can even draw pictures.)

Even Jesus felt sad at times. The Bible says Jesus wept after his friend Lazarus died. (See John 11:35.) The Bible teaches us some important lessons to remember when we feel sad. (Feel free to create your own list of promises and encouragement from the Bible. Here are a few ideas to get you started.)

1. You're never alone in your sadness because God is always with you. *"Do not be afraid or discouraged, for the LORD will personally go ahead of you. He will be with you; he will neither fail you nor abandon you"* (Deuteronomy 31:8).

2. You can lean on God for comfort when you feel sad. *"God blesses those who mourn, for they will be comforted"* (Matthew 5:4).

3. You can give your burden to God, and He will get you through it. *"Give your worries to the LORD, and he will care for you. He will never let those who are good be defeated"* (Psalm 55:22 ERV).

4. God has good plans for your life. *"'For I know the plans I have for you,' says the LORD. 'They are plans for good and not for disaster, to give you a future and a hope'"* (Jeremiah 29:11).

5. God will work everything out for your good. *"And we know that God causes everything to work together for the good of those who love God and are called according to his purpose for them"* (Romans 8:28).

Conversation Connection

» Is it okay to feel sad?

» Did Jesus ever feel sad? (The Bible tells us that Jesus experienced sadness as well. For example, He wept in John 11:35 and Luke 19:41.) Let's read a passage from Hebrews together:

While Jesus was here on earth, he offered prayers and pleadings, with a loud cry and tears, to the one who could rescue him from death. And God heard his prayers because of his deep reverence for God. Even though Jesus was God's Son, he learned obedience from the things he suffered. In this way, God qualified him as a perfect High Priest, and he became the source of eternal salvation for all those who obey him.

(Hebrews 5:7–9)

» What can we do to feel happier?

Family Fun

We're creating *sadness squashers* today! We're going to fill a container with all of our favorite things to help us feel happy when we're struggling with sadness. Create a list of items that bring you joy. Get as creative or simple as you want. You can color pictures, decorate slips of paper, or find little trinkets to represent each activity. (You may want to make two kits, one for at home and one for on the go.) Here are some ideas to get you started. List anything that helps to bring joy to create your own *joy jar*:

» Bubble bath

» Coloring

» Praying

» Talking to a friend or trusted adult

» Going to the park

» Playing a favorite game

- » Sitting in the sun
- » Playing with a friend
- » Hugging someone
- » Watching a silly show
- » Having a dance party
- » Singing silly songs
- » Worshipping God
- » Reading a book

Baking Buddies

We all feel sad at times. It's okay to cry, but we don't want to let ourselves become blubbering beasts who get stuck in their sadness because the Bible teaches us that a sad heart makes it hard to get through the day. (See Proverbs 15:13.) Jesus teaches us that even in the darkest times, we have hope. In John 16:33, He says, *"I have told you all this so that you may have peace in me. Here on earth you will have many trials and sorrows. But take heart, because I have overcome the world."* Today we are making Blubbering Blueberry Crumble Muffins to remind us that even when we are feeling blue, we can find hope, comfort, and peace in Jesus.

BLUBBERING BLUEBERRY CRUMBLE MUFFINS

Ingredients

6 tbsp. butter
¾ cup granulated sugar
2 large eggs
2 cups flour
2 tsp. baking powder
½ tsp. salt
½ cup whole milk (or alternative like oat milk)
2 tsp. vanilla extract
2 cups fresh or frozen blueberries (set ½ cup aside)

Crumble Topping

1 cup flour
⅓ cup granulated sugar
⅓ cup packed brown sugar
½ cup (1 stick) salted butter, melted
1 tsp. cinnamon

Directions

Preheat oven to 375°F. Line regular muffin pans with 12 paper liners and set aside (or make 24 mini muffins).

In a large mixing bowl, beat butter and sugar until light and fluffy.

Add eggs one at a time until fully incorporated.

In a separate bowl, whisk flour, baking powder, and salt together.

Slowly add dry ingredients to butter mixture.

Stir in milk and vanilla extract just until smooth.

If using fresh blueberries, wash and dry them with paper towels. If using frozen, rinse with warm water and then dry.

In a small bowl, toss blueberries with 1 tbsp. of flour so they're coated. This will keep them from sinking to the bottom of the cupcakes.

Gently fold 1½ cups of blueberries into the batter, reserving the remaining ½ cup for the tops.

Fill muffin cups at least ¾ full with batter, until it is all gone.

Gently press a few of the remaining blueberries into the tops of each muffin.

In a small bowl, combine melted butter, flour, sugars, and cinnamon using a fork to mix it. Spread some over the tops of each muffin (they will look like they are overflowing, but that's okay).

Bake for 20-25 minutes until lightly golden. Insert a toothpick into the center of a muffin, and if it comes out clean, they're done.

Allow them to cool in the pan on top of a cooling rack for several minutes, then remove to cooling rack. Serve them warm or save for later.

3

FEER

When I am afraid, I will put my trust and faith in You.
—Psalm 56:3 (AMP)

Fear is a natural response that can even be healthy at times—but it can also be extremely dangerous. Once it takes root in our hearts, it can be challenging to uproot fear and overcome it. It's contagious and addictive, which is one of the reasons why people flock to theaters to watch horror movies and line up to scare themselves silly at haunted houses. Fear can also cause mass hysteria. When fear consumes us, it distorts reality and alters logic and behavior.

I'll never forget watching the 1990 movie *IT* as a child. I remember being deathly afraid that a clown might come up out of the toilet or sink to get me. I'd stand as far away from the toilet as I could when I leaned over to flush—and then bolted to wash my hands as quickly as I could so I could flee from the bathroom with my heart pounding out of my chest. This went on for months! All from watching one scary movie. Crazy, right?

What are you afraid of? Spiders? Heights? Or something else?

How about your kids? Sometimes our fears are warranted, but often, they're exaggerated or illogical, like my fear of clowns in the bathroom.

However, one of the worst things we can do when our child is struggling with fear is to tell them, "There's nothing to worry about," or "Don't worry, you'll be fine." That's the same as telling an asthmatic that there's nothing to worry about when they're having an attack and can't breathe. For our kids, the fear is real even if what they're afraid of isn't.

When we're consumed by fear, we don't feel safe. So, we need help reorienting ourselves and feeling secure. As parents, we can validate and normalize the fear our kids are facing:

"I understand you're afraid right now."

"You're not alone."

"I'm here for you."

"How can I help?"

"What do you need?"

These types of statements let our children know we're with them and they can trust us.

Fear is a very common problem, even for faith-filled believers. In fact, the word *fear* is used more than five hundred times in the King James Version of the Bible. The good news is, we aren't without hope or resources to help us overcome our fear. God's Word is filled with so many promises to comfort and encourage us when we experience fear.

Parents' Prayer

Dear Lord, I pray Your perfect love would cast out all fear in our family. Fill our home with Your peace and protect our hearts and minds. In Jesus's name I pray. Amen.

Teachable Moment

We all experience fear, but we don't have to surrender to it. God has given us many promises and tools to help us overcome our fear. Today we're going to study what the Bible teaches us about fear. *Depending on your children's ages, you can modify this activity to meet their abilities.*

For younger kids, you can choose a favorite Bible story, like David and Goliath or Daniel in the lions' den. Read the Scripture or watch a video about it. Talk about how afraid David or Daniel must have been and what they did to overcome that fear. Focus on how God protected and provided for them. You can have your children draw pictures or act out the scene as well. Then, talk about what your kids are afraid of and have them act it out while also thinking about what Jesus would tell them in that situation. Take time to pray and ask God to help them not to be afraid, comfort them, and fill them with peace.

For older kids, encourage them to find passages of Scripture about fear. (For example, Joshua 1:9; Isaiah 41:10; Psalm 34:4; Psalm 56:3; 1 John 4:18.) They can copy the verses and work on memorizing them. I like to create journals with my kids where they can keep their favorite Scriptures as an easy reference in difficult circumstances. Grab a notebook and write FEAR at the top of the page. Then write out verses to help them when they're feeling afraid. Leave several pages for verses and more for journaling their thoughts, feelings, prayer requests, and testimonies of overcoming fear. You can do the same for the other struggles they face as well. They can decorate their notebooks, add drawings or pictures, and be as creative or simple as they'd like.

For teens, this is a great time to teach them how to use topical word searches in their Bibles, cross-reference Scriptures, and even utilize other Bible study tools such as concordances and commentaries to study the topic in-depth.

Conversation Connection

» Where does fear come from?

» How do you know when you're feeling afraid? (The heart speeds up, you have trouble breathing, your thoughts race, you sweat or shake, etc.)

» What can you do when you feel scared?

» Can you think of a story in the Bible in which someone was afraid? What did they do?

» How can God help us when we are afraid?

Family Fun

You're going to conquer a fear today. When we face our fears, we experience freedom. Make a list of the things you've been fearful of, then rank them from scariest to least scary. Start with the least scary fear and face it head-on. If it's spiders, go on a spider hunt. If it's heights, climb a ladder or look out the window of a tall building. If it's failure, try something new.

You can also design posters to encourage you with sayings such as, "Faith over fear," "I am fearless because God is faithful," and "I am strong and courageous." You can also create a fearless family worship playlist with songs to strengthen and encourage you whenever you feel afraid.

Baking Buddies

The fruit of the Spirit is highlighted in Galatians 5:22–23: "*But the Holy Spirit produces this kind of fruit in our lives: love, joy, peace, patience, kindness, goodness, faithfulness, gentleness, and self-control. There is no law against these things!*" As we remain in Christ, this fruit is naturally produced in our lives, and we can conquer our fears with it. Today we are going to make Fearless Fruit Oatmeal Bars to help us remember that the fruit of walking closely with Jesus is faith, not fear.

FEARLESS FRUIT OATMEAL BARS
(GLUTEN-FREE)

Ingredients

6 tbsp. unsalted butter, melted (can use coconut oil for a vegan/dairy-free substitute)

1 cup old-fashioned rolled oats (gluten-free or regular)

¾ cup 1:1 gluten-free baking flour (can also use all-purpose or whole wheat flour)

⅓ cup light brown sugar

¼ tsp. ground ginger

¼ tsp. kosher salt

2 cups blueberries* (fresh or frozen)

You can experiment with other fruit as well, but blueberry is our family's favorite

1 tsp. cornstarch

2 tbsp. lemon juice

1 tbsp. granulated sugar

Vanilla Glaze (Optional)

½ cup powdered sugar

1 tsp. pure vanilla extract

1 tbsp. milk (or milk substitute)

Directions

Preheat oven to 350°F (325°F for dark pans).

Line 8x8" cake pan with parchment paper with some paper hanging over two of the sides to make it easier to pull out the bars. (I lightly spray my pan first to keep parchment in place.)

In a medium bowl, combine flour, oats, brown sugar, ginger, and salt. Stir to combine.

Pour melted butter over mixture and use a fork to stir until evenly moistened and forming small clumps.

Press approximately half the mixture into an even layer in the bottom of your prepared cake pan. (It's okay if it takes more than half the mixture to coat the bottom of the pan; you want a solid base for the bars first.)

In a small bowl, combine fruit, cornstarch, and lemon juice. Toss to coat the fruit evenly. Then pour on top of the oat mixture in pan.

Sprinkle remaining mixture over the top. *It won't cover all the fruit, so don't worry!*

Bake 35-45 minutes, just until fruit is bubbly and topping is golden brown.

Place pan on wire rack to cool completely.

Prepare the glaze in a medium bowl by whisking powdered sugar, vanilla, and milk together until smooth. Add a bit more milk to reach desired consistency for drizzling. Use the parchment handles to remove bars from the pan. Drizzle with glaze, then slice and enjoy.

4

JEALOUSY

*A peaceful heart leads to a healthy body; jealousy
is like cancer in the bones.*
—Proverbs 14:30

Initially, King Saul loved David, but their relationship shifted when Saul became jealous of the younger man. That emotion slowly consumed Saul until it eventually led to his demise. Jealousy—or as Shakespeare penned in *Othello*, the "green-eyed monster"—rears its ugly head in all of us, but we don't have to allow it to destroy us. Jealousy breeds discontent in our own lives as we build resentment over something another person has or is. The Bible teaches us that it's like cancer in the bones. It destroys our lives physically, mentally, and spiritually.

Jealousy fills our heart when love is lacking. We see this in the definition of love from Paul:

Love is patient and kind. Love is not jealous or boastful or proud or rude. It does not demand its own way. It is not irritable, and it keeps no record of being wronged. (1 Corinthians 13:4–5)

When I love someone, I celebrate who they are and the blessings they have. I'm genuinely glad for them. However, when I don't let love lead, jealousy rears its ugly head. I become bitter about the blessings someone else receives.

I'll never forget our kids' first soccer season...honestly, it was a bit painful to watch. Our sweet son didn't seem to have a competitive bone in his body. He was happy to be on the field but had no drive to play. Our daughter struggled, but once she found where she fit in, playing defense, she thrived. Her team was extremely competitive, and they won every game. When it came time for the tournament, Kendra chose to attend my first book signing instead of participating. Still, she received a second-place trophy, along with her team.

Kendra was thrilled! She'd never received any type of award and it meant a lot to her. Her little brother, however, became jealous. Jordan was upset that he didn't receive a trophy, even though his team didn't fare well in the tournament. He whined, complained, and even tried to take Kendra's trophy.

When jealousy enters our hearts, we become competitors instead of co-laborers for Christ. It separates us and slowly destroys us from the inside out. However, by praying for and rejoicing with others, we can overcome jealousy.

Parents' Prayer

Jesus, forgive me for being jealous of others. Help me to remain humble and grateful for all the blessings in my life and to rejoice when blessings come to others. Show me the warning signs when the green-eyed monster rears its ugly head in my kids' hearts and give me the wisdom to help them navigate those situations with grace. In Jesus's name I pray. Amen.

Teachable Moment

Fill a clear cup with water. Grab a bottle of green food coloring. Explain to your kids, "Jealousy is like poison. A little bit has a big impact and pollutes our souls while rotting our body. Imagine this cup is like our bodies. What do you think will happen when we pour a drop of jealousy into it?" Add a drop of food coloring to the water in the cup. Notice how it doesn't just stay in one little place, but "infects" and affects the whole thing. Jealousy does the same to our hearts, which impacts our minds and bodies. Proverbs 14:30 teaches us: "*A peaceful heart leads to a healthy body; jealousy is like cancer in the bones.*"

Read 1 Samuel 18 with your kids. The theme of jealousy can be clearly seen here, although the story of Saul and David continues into 2 Samuel. If your kids are younger, you can look to story Bibles, videos like "1 Samuel" from the Bible Project,[1] or other online depictions of the story of these two ancient kings of Israel. Explore what triggered the jealous feelings in Saul and discuss how the jealousy eventually consumed him and led to a series of harmful choices that destroyed Saul's life.

We want to think about why we're feeling jealous and how we can change our perspective to overcome the jealousy. We need to ask ourselves, "Am I jealous because I wanted to win? I can work hard or ask others to help me while also celebrating their success, knowing I'd want them to celebrate mine. If I'm jealous because I have bad feelings toward them, I can get to the root of those bad feelings. I can focus on gratitude for what I do have. I can work on not comparing myself to anyone else."

Conversation Connection

» What does jealousy look like? Feel like?

» How did Saul's jealousy of David hurt his life?

» Tell me about a time where you've felt jealous. What did you do about it? How could you have responded differently?

» What is the antidote for jealousy? (Love, gratitude, etc.)

---

1. bibleproject.com/explore/video/1-samuel; the story of Saul and David begins at about the 4:50 mark.

Family Fun

Today, wage an epic battle to defeat the green-eyed monster, jealousy. Have as much fun with this as you want. You can dress in green and have your kids slay you with toy swords, pool noodles, or tickles. Or play hide-and-seek and find the green-eyed monster—you or a stuffed animal. You can even take turns being the monster. If you prefer, you can draw the scene, or write a short story about defeating jealousy. You can even share a progressive story where each person takes turns adding to the narrative as you tell, write, or draw it.

Baking Buddies

People often say you can become "green with envy" or refer to jealousy as the "green-eyed monster." Today, we are making Green-Eyed Matcha Monster Scones to help us remember not to let ourselves fall prey to jealousy.

GREEN-EYED MATCHA MONSTER SCONES

Ingredients

2 cups flour

1 tbsp. baking powder

½ tsp. salt

⅓ cup sugar (optional)

½ cup cold butter (cut into small cubes and keep chilled)

1 tbsp. vanilla extract

1 large egg

½ cup milk (or milk substitute such as oat milk)

1 tbsp. milk for basting the tops

½ cup dried cranberries*

½ cup white chocolate chips*

¼ cup sliced almonds

¼ cup sanding sugar

2 tbsp. matcha green tea powder (if you use sweetened powder, don't add the sugar)

Black edible marker (optional)

You can use any mix-ins you like if you don't want to use the cranberries and white chocolate. You can also replace the almonds with chocolate chips, candies, or sprinkles to make the eyes if you have a nut allergy.

Glaze Ingredients

1 cup powdered sugar
1-3 tbsp. milk
½ tsp. vanilla extract

Directions

Preheat oven to 400°F.

Grease large baking sheet and set aside.

Sift and then whisk the dry ingredients together in a medium bowl. Set aside.

Add the cold, cubed butter to the dry ingredients and use a pastry cutter to incorporate the mixture. If you don't have a pastry cutter, you can use two forks to make the crumbly mixture.

In a medium bowl, whisk together the wet ingredients.

Add the wet ingredients to the dry mixture and mix until a soft dough forms.

Fold in the white chocolate and cranberries.

Divide the dough in half. Place on a piece of waxed paper and sprinkle paper with flour. Flatten each half until the dough is approximately ½-inch thick.

Cut the dough into 8 wedges and place them on a greased baking sheet.

Use a basting brush to coat the tops with milk, then sprinkle with sanding sugar. Place 2 almond slices to look like eyes (you can use an edible marker to put a dot in the middle if you have one). You can do this for all of them, or simply sprinkle almonds over the tops of the others. Feel free to leave off if you have a nut allergy. Consider sprinkles or candies instead.

Bake for 12-15 minutes, just until the edges are golden brown.

To make the glaze, whisk the powdered sugar, vanilla extract, and 1 tbsp. milk until smooth. Add additional tablespoons of milk as needed to reach desired consistency. I prefer a thick glaze for this recipe.

5

GRIEF

The LORD is close to the brokenhearted;
he rescues those whose spirits are crushed.
—Psalm 34:18

Death touches all of us at some point in our lives. As a teenager, I lost my father and grandfather within a few months of each other. I also spent years providing grief counseling to children, teens, and adults in my professional career. You'd think I'd have been an expert in navigating grief and loss issues, but I wasn't prepared for the grief my five-year-old daughter would face with the loss of her great-grandmother in 2018.

Kendra didn't know her great-grandmother all that well because she hadn't spent a significant amount of time with her. Yet the loss hit her with unexpected force. Kendra wept for her dad's grandmother constantly. She clung to the only photo she had of her and began to seek deeper answers about death and heaven.

Despite my experience in providing grief counseling to other families, as a mom, I still felt a bit unprepared for how to navigate my own daughter's grief. I'll never forget the horror that coursed through my veins when

I heard my sweet girl talk about wanting to die so she could go to heaven and be with Great Grandma Trent. Fear gripped me as I fought for the right words to say to help her in those devastating moments. Just when I thought we'd moved past the grief, it would come back full force, triggered by a thought or a memory—or seemingly nothing at all.

It can be overwhelming to try to help our kids walk through their grief, especially as we're attempting to muddle through our own. Grief is a journey as unique as each of us. There is no right or wrong way to grieve and no magical timeframe. It can be an unpredictable tempest tossing us to and fro as we desperately cling to whatever we can—which is why we need to anchor our hope in Jesus and teach our kids to do the same. When we hold onto Christ, our grief can never veer us off course.

When our daughter grieved for her great-grandmother, we took the time to hold her and validate her feelings. We taught her to pray and studied what the Bible revealed about heaven, as well as the hope we have as followers of Christ. We encouraged art and journaling as artistic expressions and outlets for her grief, and in time, she was able to move forward from the loss.

Sweet friend, wherever you may be on your own journey, I want you to know that there is hope for you and your kiddos too. You're not alone.

Parents' Prayer

Holy Spirit, comfort us in our time of grief. Equip me with the words to speak and the actions to take to help my children process their sorrow. We choose to look to Jesus to anchor our hearts as we navigate this difficult season. In Jesus's name I pray. Amen.

Teachable Moment

Grief is more than an emotion; it's a process of healing. We grieve when people die, but we can also grieve the loss of what we thought life might look like, or the loss of friendships, jobs, pets, and more.

While there is no right or wrong way to grieve, there are healthy and unhealthy coping skills we may use. Unhealthy coping might include withdrawing from others, turning away from God, eating when we're not hungry in an effort to feed our feelings, or using harmful substances to try to numb our pain. Such actions hurt us and others. So, we want to focus on building and using healthy coping skills to overcome our grief.

We are going to create a *Coping Kit* to help us as we grieve. Let's begin by listing all of the healthy ways we can share and deal with our grief.

>> Make a memory box and fill it with pictures, trinkets, and stories to help remember the person you lost or the season you're mourning.

>> Start a journal to draw pictures or write to express thoughts, feelings, and questions.

>> Create a promise poster filled with Scriptures in which the promises of God can help us through our grieving process. Here are a few: Psalm 23; Psalm 34:18; Psalm 73:26; Proverbs 3:5–6; Isaiah 49:13; Matthew 5:4; Luke 6:21; John 11:25–26; Romans 8:18; Romans 15:13; 2 Corinthians 1:3–4; 2 Corinthians 4:17–18; 1 Thessalonians 4:13–14; Revelation 21:4.

>> Turn the promises into prayers. For example, referring to Proverbs 3:5–6, you could pray, "God, help me to trust in You with all my heart and not lean on my own understanding. Give me eyes to see You in the midst of my sorrow and direct my path. Amen."

>> Make a list of people you can talk to when you're feeling sad or overwhelmed. Include their contact information (phone number, email, etc.).

>> Creative expressions such as coloring, drawing, painting, writing poems or songs, or doing arts and crafts projects can be very cathartic in the grieving process.

» Go on a nature walk. Focus on your five senses and enjoy the wonder and beauty of God's creation around you. Begin to praise God and thank Him for the gifts that surround you. "Thank You, God, for the beauty and sweet aroma of flowers. Thank You for painting the sky with clouds and sunsets. Thank You for the songs of the birds..."

» Write a letter to your loved one who's passed, sharing your thoughts and feelings.

» Listen to your favorite worship songs and sing praises to Jesus at the top of your lungs.

» For older kids, write out a list of questions and research the answers (Why do people die? Why do bad things happen to good people? Why didn't God heal them?) Don't let your own lack of knowledge scare you. Talk to your pastor, research on the Internet, pray, and teach your kids that it's okay to contemplate a question for which there may not be an answer. It can be hard to comprehend the ways of our infinite God with our limited human minds. But even when we have unanswered questions, we can cling to God's promises and our knowledge that *"God is love"* (1 John 4:8), and He is faithful. (See 2 Thessalonians 3:3.)

Conversation Connection

» What are some unhealthy ways people sometimes cope with grief?

» What are some healthy ways we can cope with our grief?

» What does the Bible teach us about grief? Did Jesus experience grief?

» What is the hardest part about what you're feeling right now?

» How can you help a friend who's struggling with grief? What do you wish your friends and family would do for you in your grief?

Family Fun

Grief is tricky for families. Often, when our kids are grieving, so are we. Sometimes it can help to throw a little celebration of life for your family to rejoice over the life your loved one had and imagine the party thrown in heaven when they returned to the arms of their Savior. Throw a small party in honor of your loved one. This also works if you are grieving the loss of a friendship or coping with a different type of transition in your life. You can make the event as simple or as elaborate as you want, but take time to share memories and thank God for that blessing in your life. Teach your kids that life is meant to be celebrated. The Bible teaches us:

Always be full of joy. Never stop praying. Whatever happens, always be thankful. This is how God wants you to live in Christ Jesus.
(1 Thessalonians 5:16–18 ERV)

Rejoice in the Lord always. Again I will say, rejoice!
(Philippians 4:4 NKJV)

Baking Buddies

Grief can make us feel gooey and unsure. Sometimes it can be hard to get out of bed or we can feel stuck like glue—unsure of what to do next or how to move forward. Today we are going to make Grieving Gooey Butter Cake to help us remember that God is the glue that holds us together when we feel like we're falling apart. And He promises to be with us and help us through the hard things in life. *"My health may fail, and my spirit may grow weak, but God remains the strength of my heart; he is mine forever"* (Psalm 73:26).

GRIEVING GOOEY BUTTER CAKE
(GLUTEN-FREE)

Ingredients

1 pkg. yellow cake mix (can be regular or gluten-free)
1 large egg
½ cup melted butter

Filling

8 oz. cream cheese, softened
½ cup melted butter
2 large eggs
2 cups powdered sugar
1 tsp. vanilla extract

Directions

Preheat oven to 350°F.

Lightly grease 9x13" baking pan and set aside.

In your stand mixer bowl or other large bowl, combine cake mix, 1 egg, and ½ cup of butter and mix well for approximately two minutes with electric mixer or paddle attachment of the stand mixer.

Press mixture evenly into bottom of your greased pan.

In a large bowl, beat cream cheese until smooth.

Add ½ cup butter, 2 eggs, and vanilla. Beat until combined.

Add powdered sugar and mix well.

Spread filling evenly over cake batter.

Bake 40-50 minutes. Center should still be a little gooey, so don't over-bake. Bottom will be golden brown, and the top will be mostly set with a little jiggle.

6

OPPOSITION/DEFIANCE

Children, always obey your parents, for this pleases the Lord.
—Colossians 3:20

Some children are naturally born more with more compliant personalities. I wish I could say I had those children...but I don't. No, I have strong, independent, passionate kids who seem to like to question everything—and struggle with not being in complete control.

How about you? Maybe your child pushes beyond strong-willed more to the oppositional end of the spectrum. These kids can be the most draining and difficult to work with and may even require some professional help. If that's the case, don't be afraid to reach out to a counselor. It can make a huge difference!

Regardless of whether your child submits to your authority or boldly defies you, we all face this battle with our kids once in a while. Even God experienced it with Adam and Eve. They literally had the world yet chose to break the one rule God set for their own protection. And because of their defiance, we all wrestle with sin.

When our kids learn to obey us, they also learn the importance of obeying God. Jesus will never be Lord of our lives if we don't live an obedient life. This is why we teach our kids to obey all the way, right away, and with a good attitude. Lacking in any of these leads to rebellion, and the Bible teaches us, "*Rebellion is as sinful as witchcraft, and stubbornness as bad as worshiping idols*" (1 Samuel 15:23).

Typically, when a child is struggling with oppositional or defiant behavior, there are things we can do as parents to better support them. For example, clear expectations and consequences should be written out and posted somewhere.

Help prepare your kids for transitions to avoid a power struggle. Let them know what you expect of them by saying things like, "In ten minutes, you'll need to come inside and finish your chores." Use timers or visual aids such as marking a clock with tape. Also, acknowledge and demonstrate empathy for their feelings. Try to use positive directives instead of negative commands or questions to minimize pushback.

When you tell your kids all of the things they *can* do instead of what they *can't* do, you'll encounter far less resistance. Try to give them choices (that you can live with) whenever possible, and be sure to praise your child often for obedience.

Finally, do not allow them to engage you in a power struggle. *You* are the parent, so *you* are in charge. Remember, we don't negotiate with terrorists, and we don't want to argue or get sucked into their emotional responses. Keep calm and stand firm. With consistency and a lot of prayer, you'll begin to see improvement.

Parents' Prayer

God, please help me to be patient. Show me how to instill compliance in my children and guide us to strengthen our heart-to-heart connection. In Jesus's name I pray. Amen.

Teachable Moment

Is defiance really a big deal? If your kids are younger, the story of Adam and Eve is a great starting place for exploring the concept of defiance. Pick your favorite children's storybook Bible and read the story of Adam and Eve. Ask them if Adam and Eve obeyed God (no) and what happened because they were defiant. Depending on their ages, you can even explore the concept of how Adam and Eve's disobedience has negatively impacted your own and your kids' lives. Another option is to study the story of Jonah and how his defiance led to three days in the belly of a fish. Be sure to point out how merciful God was when Jonah repented and chose to obey God.

Pick a Scripture verse about obeying your parents and work on memorizing it together. Colossians 3:20 or Exodus 20:12 are good places to start.

If your kids are older, teach them how to do a keyword search in their Bibles. Look for words like *submission, humility,* and *humble.* Pride tends to be a major contributing factor in rebellion, opposition, or defiance, so you can also dive into the warnings and consequences of pride if you wish. Look at the verses and discuss what we learn about the dangers of opposition and defiance through those passages. Ask your kids to explain in their own words why submission is so important in the kingdom of God and how that translates to our daily lives.

Conversation Connection

» What does it mean to submit to someone?

» Why is submission important in our relationship with Jesus? What about in our family relationships?

» How does defiance hurt us and those we care about?

» What's one way you struggle with defiance? How can you change it?

Family Fun

Today, we're going to play the Mother, May I? game. Mom stands at a *finish line* while the kids line up at the *starting line*. Each person takes turns asking, "Mother, may I…" The kids can have fun and be creative with these requests—asking if they can go forward three steps, take a spinning leap, hop backward four times, do jumping jacks, etc. "Mother" gets to say, "Yes, you may" or "No, you may not." Explain that Colossians 3:20 tells us, *"Children, always obey your parents, for this pleases the Lord."* Then give your children a chance to be in charge of the game.

Baking Buddies

The Bible warns us about defying God and the authorities He has placed in our lives:

> *Everyone must submit to governing authorities. For all authority comes from God, and those in positions of authority have been placed there by God. So anyone who rebels against authority is rebelling against what God has instituted, and they will be punished.*   (Romans 13:1–2)

Just as Adam and Eve's defiance of God's rules led to unnecessary pain and suffering for all of us, our own defiance can have long-lasting consequences as well. This is why we don't want to defy our parents or others in authority. Today we're making Don't be Defiant Gravity-Defying Cake to remind us that the effects of our choices spill out into every area of our lives and affect others as well.

DON'T BE DEFIANT
GRAVITY-DEFYING CAKE

Ingredients

3 cups all-purpose flour (plus more for dusting)
1 cup (2 sticks) unsalted butter, softened to room temperature
2 cups granulated sugar
4 large eggs
1½ tsp. baking powder
Pinch of salt
1 cup whole milk
1 ½ tsp. pure vanilla extract
¾ cup rainbow sprinkles

Frosting

1 ½ cups (3 sticks) unsalted butter, softened
6 cups powdered sugar
1 tbsp. pure vanilla extract
2-4 tbsp. heavy cream or whole milk
Pinch of salt

Gravity-Defying Effect

3 oz. white fondant icing*
Powdered sugar for dusting
Lots of rainbow sprinkles for decorating

Corn syrup for brushing
1 bent metal straw (or plastic straw with a wooden skewer)
Small paper treat bag
If you don't want to use fondant, you can coat the straw with melted white chocolate and cover with sprinkles instead.

Directions

Preheat oven to 350°F. Place a 9" round cake pan over parchment paper and trace two circles; these will line the bottoms of the pans for easy removal. Cut them out.

Spray two 9" round cake pans with cooking spray and then line the bottoms with the circles of parchment paper. Spray again with cooking spray and then sprinkle some flour into each pan and shake to dump out any excess flour.

In the bowl of your stand mixer (or large bowl with electric hand mixer), beat butter and sugar on medium-high for 2-3 minutes, until fluffy.

Beat in the eggs one at a time.

In a medium bowl, whisk together the flour, baking powder, and salt.

Measure out the milk and stir the vanilla into the milk.

Gradually add in a little of the flour mixture followed by a little of the milk mixture until everything is incorporated.

Use a spatula to gently fold in the sprinkles.

Divide the batter between the two prepared pans and smooth the tops with your spatula. Bake 30-40 minutes, until a toothpick inserted into the centers comes out clean.

Allow the cakes to cool in the pans for about five minutes before turning them out onto a wire rack to cool completely. (*Be careful with the hot pans.*)

To make the frosting, sift the powdered sugar into a large bowl and set aside.

Beat the softened butter in a large bowl with your stand mixer (whisk attachment) or electric hand mixer until light and fluffy (4-6 minutes so it gets light and airy).

Gradually add in powdered sugar and continue beating until it's all incorporated. Scrape down the sides of the bowl with a spatula as needed.

Once the butter and powdered sugar have all been combined, add in the vanilla, salt, and 1 tablespoon of the milk/cream. Beat in additional tablespoons of milk/cream one at a time until you reach the desired consistency (it should be thick enough to ice the cake with).

To assemble your cake, place the first layer on a cake stand and spread about a cup of frosting on the top of the layer. Place the second layer on top.

Frost the rest of the cake.

To make your cake gravity-defying, dust your counter with powdered sugar and roll out the fondant into a long rectangle, approximately 2x8".

Wrap the fondant around the straw, but leave the bottom 2" or so bare. Pinch the seam to seal it to the straw, then roll it between your fingers to smooth it out. (*Don't forget to insert the skewer into the straw for stability if you are using a plastic one*).

Rub or brush the fondant straw with corn syrup, then roll it in the sprinkles and press so they stick to the straw. Place it in the fridge on a small plate to firm up while you do the next step.

Mark a spot on the cake that's off of the center for the straw to go into. Then, pour your sprinkles so they flow from that spot and down one side of the cake.

Take the straw from the fridge and insert it into the cake in the spot you marked.

Place the open end of the treat sack over the bent part of the straw, using a dab of corn syrup to adhere it if necessary. This makes it look like the sprinkles are pouring out of the bag! Refrigerate until ready to serve.

1

HATRED

But whoever hates their brother or sister is in darkness.
They live in darkness. They don't know where they are going,
*because the **darkness has made them blind.***
—1 John 2:11 (ERV)

What starts out as a small hurt or offense often grows into outright hatred if we aren't careful to guard our hearts. This danger is present even for our young children. My daughter was three when a preschool teacher grabbed her arm and attempted to pull her back inside the classroom after recess. Kendra's sweet little heart was deeply wounded by this incident. The teacher didn't leave a physical mark, but the situation left a mark on her soul.

Despite leaving the school shortly thereafter and processing the situation with her, Kendra held onto unforgiveness. We prayed for the teacher and talked with Kendra about the importance of forgiveness, but the incident stayed with her for years. Finally, we had to address the root of bitterness that was growing to hatred in her heart.

It's so easy for us to allow hurts to fester instead of heal—and before we realize it, hatred has burned a hole in our heart. This is especially true when we've been deeply wounded by someone, or repeatedly hurt. I've battled this strong emotion as well, toward my own father.

After many years of events that don't bear mentioning here, my father became gravely ill just before I graduated from high school. He happened to be living across the state in the same city that was home to the college I planned to attend. He wrote a card explaining how he was too sick to make it to my high school graduation but looked forward to seeing me once I moved. I was so hurt and angry because of our past that I threw the card in the garbage. My dad died within a month of sending that card.

At his funeral, I felt no sorrow. I shed no tears. In fact, it wasn't until several years later— after giving my heart to the Lord— that I realized just how consumed by hatred I'd become. I'll never forget reading the scathing words I had written about my dad in my senior project. It was like looking into the window of my broken soul.

I repented and asked God to heal my heart right then. And He did. I'm now able to reflect on my childhood and remember the joy alongside the sorrow. I see my father through the lens of his own pain and brokenness instead of through my own. And while I no longer have his last letter, I focus on his message that he gave his life to the Lord, which assures me that we will be reunited one day in eternal salvation.

Through these experiences, both mine and my daughter's, I've learned that hurt can easily turn to hate if we don't guard our hearts. Proverbs 4:23 warns, "*Guard your heart above all else, for it determines the course of your life.*"

Parents' Prayer

Father God, heal my heart of all my hurts. Forgive me for harboring any hate in my heart. Reveal the source of any hatred in my children's hearts and help them to heal as well. In Jesus's name I pray. Amen.

Teachable Moment

Hurt becomes hate if we don't allow it to heal. Genesis 4 tells us the story of two brothers, Cain and Abel. Abel did what was pleasing to the

Lord, offering the first and best lambs from his flock as a gift to God. (See verse 4.) But Cain only *"presented some of his crops as a gift"* (verse 3)—and the Lord didn't accept his gift. When Cain became angry and jealous of his brother, God warned him, *"You will be accepted if you do what is right. But if you refuse to do what is right, then watch out! Sin is crouching at the door, eager to control you. But you must subdue it and be its master"* (Genesis 4:7).

Cain allowed hatred to consume him and ended up killing his own brother and then lying to God about it. (See verses 8–9.) You may be thinking, *What does it matter if I hate someone if I don't plan to murder them?* However, the Bible warns us that harboring hatred in our heart is no different than murder: *"Anyone who hates another brother or sister is really a murderer at heart. And you know that murderers don't have eternal life within them"* (1 John 3:15).

Hate is a powerful emotion, but there's one emotion more powerful than any other—*and that is love.*

Love never gives up, never loses faith, is always hopeful, and endures through every circumstance. (1 Corinthians 13:7)

We overcome hate with love. The Bible teaches us, *"Hatred causes arguments, but love overlooks all wrongs"* (Proverbs 10:12 ERV). The Bible also teaches us that love comes from God.

*But anyone who does not love does not know God, for **God is love**. God showed us how much he loved us by sending his one and only Son into the world so that we might have eternal life through him.*
(1 John 4:8–9)

Jesus gives us clear instructions on how to behave toward those who hurt us, saying, *"But to you who are willing to listen, I say, love your enemies! Do good to those who hate you. Bless those who curse you. Pray for those who hurt you"* (Luke 6:27–28).

Today we're going to start the process of healing our hearts by journaling. (If your kids are too young to write, encourage them to draw pictures to express how they feel.) We're going to pour out our hearts to God, and then we're going to begin to pray for the people who have hurt us. We'll pray for them every day until we can think about them with love and forgiveness in our hearts.

» Grab a new notebook and on the first page, write out the following Scripture: "*Love is patient and kind. Love is not jealous or boastful or proud or rude. It does not demand its own way. It is not irritable, and it keeps no record of being wronged*" (1 Corinthians 13:4–5).

» Leave a few pages blank at the front for additional Scriptures. For young children, you can draw or cut out and glue paper hearts and write simple words from the Scripture. Write "LOVE IS" on the top of the page. Kids can draw pictures to help them remember what the words mean and can put big X's beside what love is not.

» Then begin pouring out your heart to God in the journal. Encourage your child to share the hurt and then take time to pray and ask God to heal it. Be sure to end with "I choose to forgive _____" and pray for specific blessings for that person. (*Refer to chapter 13 if you need additional assistance with forgiveness.*)

Conversation Connection

» Where does hate come from?

» What is the opposite of hate?

» How can we defeat hate?

» Have you ever battled hate or are you doing that now? Let's talk about the hurt and ask God to heal our hearts. We can begin to heal by praying for the person who's hurt us. Anytime that hate tries to come back, we can pray for the person again and again until we have nothing left but love in our hearts for them, as Jesus commands.

Family Fun

Today we're going to play Toss Hate Over the Gate. Grab a ball or a bunch of balls and place something in the yard to toss the balls over. It can even be a cardboard box. Talk about how Jesus wants us to toss our hate to Him so He can fill us with love. Each player takes a turn with the ball and shares a hate they've held in their heart. (This could be toward a person or toward an activity they don't like to do.) Say, "God, I give You my hate and ask You to fill me with Your love instead." Then toss the ball over the gate. Keep going until you've all emptied your hearts of hate, then move on to the delicious baking treat.

If you're doing this activity in inclement weather or simply prefer to do a craft instead, you can cut out a paper heart from construction paper. Save the outer edge of the paper and glue it onto a different colored piece of paper. Along the edges write or draw pictures of things that represent your struggles with hatred. On the heart inside, write *God is love.* Hang it on the wall as a reminder to pray every time you see it so God can heal your heart and fill it with His love instead of hate.

Baking Buddies

Hatred hardens our hearts, but the love of God fills the empty places inside us and softens our hearts toward Him and others. Today we're going to make Loving Lime Sugar Cookies to remind us to allow God to soften our hearts with love, which will brighten and refresh our lives just as lime refreshes our tongues. We're going to put white chocolate chips in the cookies to help us remember to keep our hearts pure by forgiving those who hurt us, just as Jesus commands.

LOVING LIME SUGAR COOKIES

Ingredients

½ cup unsalted butter, softened
¼ cup granulated sugar
¼ cup light brown sugar
1 large egg
½ tsp. vanilla extract
1 tsp. key lime zest
2 ½ tbsp. key lime juice
1 ½ cups all-purpose flour
½ tsp. baking soda
½ tsp. salt
½ cup white chocolate chips

Glaze

¾ cup powdered sugar
1-1½ tbsp. key lime juice
Lime zest to sprinkle on top

Directions

Line a lightly colored baking sheet with parchment paper.

Take one lime and zest it by grating the peel into a small bowl. *If you don't have a zester, you can use a cheese grater. Be careful not to zest off the white part, which is bitter.*

Slice the lime in half and squeeze the juice of both halves into another small bowl, preferably with a citrus press to avoid seeds. *If you don't have a citrus press, you can use a strainer to strain the seeds before measuring out the lime juice.* Set aside.

In a small bowl, combine flour, baking soda, and salt and whisk together. Set aside.

In the bowl of your stand mixer or another large bowl, beat butter and sugars together until smooth and creamy.

Add egg, vanilla, lime juice, and zest and mix until combined.

Mix in dry ingredients.

Fold in white chocolate chips. Dough will be wet and sticky.

Cover and refrigerate dough for 30-60 minutes until chilled.

Preheat oven to 375°F.

Use a cookie scoop to scoop rounded balls of dough onto prepared baking sheet, placing cookies approximately 2" apart. *Don't over-handle the dough as you want it to remain chilled. If it becomes too soft, you can place the tray in the fridge for 10 minutes to firm up again.*

Bake 7-8 minutes. Don't overbake. Cookies will remain lightly colored but will not appear glossy and doughy.

Allow cookies to cool on sheet for 4-5 minutes before transferring to a wire rack to finish cooling.

Mix powdered sugar and 1 tbsp. lime juice in a small bowl or liquid measuring cup. Whisk to combine. It should be thick enough not to run off the cookie, but still a scooping/drizzling consistency. Add more lime juice if needed to reach desired consistency.

Pour approximately one teaspoon of glaze on each cookie and then sprinkle with a little lime zest.

Allow to set so icing hardens, then enjoy.

8

ANXIETY/WORRY

Be anxious for nothing, but in everything by prayer and supplication,
with thanksgiving, let your requests be made known to God; and the
peace of God, which surpasses all understanding, will guard your
hearts and minds through Christ Jesus.
—Philippians 4:6–7 (NKJV)

Anxiety in our kids can take many forms: irritability, exhaustion, clinginess, physical issues like stomach pains and headaches, emotional outbursts, withdrawal, avoidance, trouble concentrating, inattention, or even twenty questions. It can be difficult to recognize sometimes because of the many forms it takes. But if you notice a pattern of these behaviors, addressing worry is always a good place to start.

During my years of providing counseling to children, teens, and adults, anxiety was the No. 1 issue my clients faced. I worked with many kids as young as four who struggled with some form of anxiety disorder. Anxiety is multifaceted, and if you are seriously struggling, or your child is, I encourage you to seek out the help of a professional counselor. The resources in this book are meant to provide additional biblical support as you navigate challenges within your home or homeschool life, but not to replace everything else.

We all experience anxiety throughout our lives, regardless of whether it reaches a level that warrants clinical intervention. This is not a new struggle, as the Bible is filled with Scriptures encouraging us not to worry and to be anxious for nothing. Anxiety is rooted in fear—fear of the unknown, fear of not being in control, and fear of how others will respond.

Our daughter Kendra began battling anxiety when she was four or five. She struggled with perfectionism, emotional outbursts, and difficulty concentrating. My husband wrestled with how to respond to her worries because he didn't understand them. Her responses made no logical sense to him, which frustrated him.

As parents, we often feel helpless when our child is struggling with worry and anxiety because it's hard to convince them that the thing they're worrying about won't actually happen or is nothing to stress over. We've got to acknowledge the struggle is real for them and validate their feelings. We need to normalize their experience, support them as they learn coping skills to overcome the fear, and pray diligently for them as they learn to rest in God's peace and His promises along the way.

Parents' Prayer

Jesus, Prince of Peace, fill our hearts and minds with Your peace that surpasses all understanding. Equip me with the tools and words to help my children overcome anxiety and trust completely in You. Amen.

Teachable Moment

Anxiety stems from fear or worry. Today we are going to learn how to become fear fighters! Fear spreads like wildfire if we allow it to remain unguarded in our hearts and minds.

Fear Fighting Strategy #1

Most Likely Scenario Game

Fear often feeds off worst-case scenarios. While it's true that something may be remotely *possible*, like an asteroid hitting our house, many of our fears are also extremely unlikely. So when we have a fear that's bugging us, we can say our worst fear out loud and decide if it's a *worst case, best case,* or *most likely case* scenario. For example, a *worst-case scenario* would be an asteroid hitting our house while we slept, which would result in all of us going to heaven together to be with Jesus. *Best case* would be no asteroid at all. The *most likely* case is no asteroid hitting our house. According to NASA, it's extremely unlikely that an asteroid would hit the earth at all, and the chances of it hitting our house out of every place else on earth makes it even more unlikely. Besides, I'm sure NASA keeps track of asteroids and would warn people if one were headed for the earth!

Fear Fighting Strategy #2

Calming Caddy Creation

Fear is going to strike, but it doesn't have to succeed. We can arm ourselves with coping strategies to help us calm down when anxiety or worry hit us. Create a list of different coping strategies you can use when you feel anxious. Practice them when you're calm so they become like second nature and are more easily implemented in times of stress.

Deep breathing exercises make a big difference when anxiety strikes. Practice breathing in slowly through the nose and gradually exhaling through the mouth. For young kids, have them imagine they are holding a birthday cupcake with a candle in the palm of their hand. Slowly breathe in the delicious smell of the cupcake, then slowly blow out the candle.

Progressive muscle relaxation exercises are another good way to combat anxiety. Tense and release muscle groups from toe to head while deeply breathing. We tend to carry stress in our bodies and don't realize it, so this helps to relieve the tension.

Other ideas to include in your calming caddy include: take a bubble bath or hot shower; listen to worship music; draw, color or paint; journal; talk to someone; hug yourself to calm your core or hug someone you love; recite positive affirmations such as, "I am safe," "It will be okay," and "God is with me"; look out the window at nature; go for a walk; watch a funny movie; and dance, exercise, or play a favorite game.

Fear Fighting Strategy #3

Sword of the Spirit

Ephesians 6:10–18 teaches us how to put on the whole armor of God so we can stand firm against the strategies of the devil. Verse 17 says, *"Put on salvation as your helmet, and take the sword of the Spirit, which is the word of God."* This tells us that we slay the lies of the enemy with the truth of God's Word. Create a journal or poster with verses to stand on when feeling anxious. Here are some verses to get you started: Deuteronomy 31:6; Psalm 27:1; Psalm 34:4; Psalm 46:1; Psalm 55:22; Psalm 91; Psalm 94:19; Proverbs 29:25; Isaiah 41:13–14; Matthew 6:34; Mark 4:39–40; Luke 12:22–26; John 14:27; Philippians 4:6–7; 2 Timothy 1:7; 1 John 4:18.

Conversation Connection

» What are you most worried about? Why?

» How do you know when you're feeling worried or anxious?

» What makes the worry or anxiety worse?

» Can you think of a time where you felt anxious or worried but were able to overcome that feeling? If so, how did you do it? What helped?

» What can you do to feel better when you feel anxious or worried?

Family Fun

Today we're going to be fear fighters! Let's make our own fear fighting squad! Depending on your kids' ages and interests, consider a sword fight with cardboard swords, act out a play demonstrating how a biblical hero overcame a fearful situation—such as Moses approaching Pharaoh, Esther going before the king, Peter walking on water, David fighting Goliath, or Daniel in the lions' den—and then act out how you conquer your own fears. You can draw, write or illustrate anxiety triggers and then turn them into targets and shoot nerf balls at them. You could also draw or dress up in the armor of God and discuss how it protects you every day. (See Ephesians 6:10–18.) Regardless of what you choose, have fun as a family, and affirm that you will fight the fears together. Let your kids know that with God on your side, you can't lose! Jesus says, *"I have told you all this so that you may have peace in me. Here on earth you will have many trials and sorrows. But take heart, because I have overcome the world"* (John 16:33).

Baking Buddies

Worry and anxiety rob us of many blessings in everyday life. We miss out on the present because we are fretting about the future. Matthew 6:34 (MSG) says, *"Give your entire attention to what God is doing right now, and don't get worked up about what may or may not happen tomorrow. God will help you deal with whatever hard things come up when the time comes."*

Today we are making Worry-Free FUNnel Cakes to remind us not to worry so we don't miss the fun and blessings each day can bring. Even if things look really bad right now, God promises He will work it all out for our good: *"And we know that God causes everything to work together for the good of those who love God and are called according to his purpose for them"* (Romans 8:28).

WORRY-FREE FUNNEL CAKES

Ingredients

Vegetable or canola oil for frying (1/2" deep in large skillet or pan)
1 ½ cups milk
¼ cup granulated sugar
2 large eggs
1 tsp. pure vanilla extract
2 cups all-purpose flour
1 ½ tsp. baking powder
1 tsp. ground cinnamon (optional)
¼ tsp. ground nutmeg (optional)
¼ tsp. salt
*Toppings of choice – powdered sugar, fresh fruit, whipped topping, or caramel or chocolate sauce

Warning: This recipe requires extremely hot oil, which can be dangerous for children. Parents should be the ones to place cakes in and out of oil to avoid burns. Kids can have fun with topping their cake and helping mix the batter.
Makes approximately 12 funnel cakes. You can cut the recipe in half if you don't want that much batter.

Directions

Use a large skillet or pot and fill halfway with oil, approximately ½" deep. Place over medium heat. You want the oil to reach a temperature of

350°F (177°C). Use a cooking thermometer to check temperature if you have one.

While oil is heating, make the batter. In a medium bowl, whisk together flour, baking powder, cinnamon, nutmeg, and salt. Set aside.

Use a large mixing bowl to whisk together milk, granulated sugar, eggs, and vanilla extract until combined.

Add the dry ingredients to the wet ones and whisk just until fully incorporated.

Line a baking sheet or plate with paper towels to dry excess oil off cakes.

If you have a squeeze bottle, you can pour the batter into it; otherwise you can use a funnel or even a liquid measuring cup to pour the batter into the oil once it has reached 350°F. *If using a funnel, be sure to close the bottom end by placing a finger securely under it before you pour batter into it.*

Carefully pour approximately ¼-1/3 cup of batter into the oil using a circular motion and overlapping the batter.

Cook for 1-2 minutes until golden brown on the bottom, then use tongs or a flat spatula to carefully flip the funnel cake over. Cook for an additional 1-2 minutes.

Carefully remove funnel cake from oil with the tongs or spatula and place on paper towels. Allow to cool slightly, then sprinkle with powdered sugar or toppings of choice and enjoy.

Repeat until everyone has a funnel cake.

9

DEPRESSION

*He heals the brokenhearted and binds up their wounds [healing their
pain and comforting their sorrow].*
—Psalm 147:3 (AMP)

Depression is another issue for which I have spent a lot of my time counseling children and teens. Some kids experience a general, constant sadness, while others experience it in bouts or even just in certain seasons. All children will experience sadness at times throughout their lives, but not everyone will experience depression, which occurs when that sadness significantly impacts areas of our lives. In your child or teen, it might manifest as behavioral problems, feelings of hopelessness, loss of interest in fun activities, low energy and tiredness, mood changes and irritability, or changes in eating and sleeping habits.

After giving birth to my first child, I battled postpartum depression. Because of my education and experience, I recognized the signs and was able to implement coping strategies and communicate my needs to my husband. And when we had our second child, we were both better prepared for the symptoms, which made them so much more manageable. It wasn't easy, but understanding what we were facing and having the right tools helped us cope and overcome the depression quicker.

By teaching our kids to understand and recognize symptoms of depression and how to implement coping strategies, they can learn to manage it throughout their lives. It's also important to normalize the struggle and encourage them to ask for help when it's needed. We want our kids to know we're a safe place when they are struggling. We also want to teach them how to turn to Jesus in those dark and difficult times, so they know they are never alone. There's reason to hope even if a situation seems hopeless.

If your child is experiencing symptoms of depression, it's always a good idea to take them to see their primary care physician or pediatrician to rule out any underlying medical issues and explore treatment options. However, as a parent, you should trust your own discernment and know that it's okay to seek a second opinion, or to choose the least invasive treatment options. Don't be afraid to ask questions and make sure you're comfortable with the recommendations.

If your child expresses thoughts of suicide or engages in self-harming behavior, seek immediate professional help. The National Suicide Prevention Lifeline is a free resource available 24/7: Call 988, which was recently implemented to be easier to remember than the old toll-free number, 800-273-8255. Or in case of an emergency, call 911.

Parents' Prayer

Holy Spirit, comfort us. Teach us to recognize and overcome these depressive symptoms. Renew our hope and help us put our trust more fully in You. Protect our children from the lies of the enemy that bind them in hopelessness and sorrow. Lift them out of the pits of despair and strengthen them with Your joy. In Jesus's name I pray. Amen.

Teachable Moment

We all feel sad sometimes, but depression is a medical condition where that sadness starts to have a big impact on your life. Depression includes feeling sad, empty, or irritable and often involves losing interest in activities you normally enjoy, feeling bad about yourself, feeling hopeless about the future, having trouble sleeping or wanting to sleep a lot, being tired and having no energy, and experiencing changes in eating habits, such as overeating or not wanting to eat at all. It may also cause thoughts about dying.

If you or someone in your family is struggling with depression, it may help to know that you're not alone. Depression is not a new struggle; in fact, we find many people throughout the Bible who suffered with depression, including Moses (Numbers 11:10–15), Elijah (1 Kings 19:1–18), King David (Psalm 32:3–4, Psalm 51), Job (Job 30:16–31), and Jonah (Jonah 4:1–11), just to name a few. And the Bible is filled with promises about the hope and joy we have in relationship with Jesus.

It's always important to guard our hearts and our minds, but especially when we are feeling depressed. What we watch, hear, and think about will either fill us with hope or empty us in despair. We're going to do several activities to help fill us with hope.

Physical activity, exercise, and sunshine are all powerful tools to help us feel better when battling depression. There are also other enjoyable activities that don't require a ton of energy or planning. It helps to have a plan in place so you don't have to try to figure things out when you're already fighting depressive symptoms.

These activities will likely be too overwhelming to do all at once if your child is struggling with serious depression, so don't be afraid to space them out and do as they are able:

» Create an uplifting worship playlist to listen to whenever we're struggling with depression.

» Write out a list of movies or videos we can watch that fill us with hope.

» Make a list of encouraging Scriptures to hold on to in times of despair.

» Jot down a list of activities that can help when we feel depressed.

Conversation Connection

» What is the difference between sadness and depression?

» What are some of the ways you can tell someone might be experiencing depression?

» What can you do if you're feeling depressed?

» What kinds of help are available for kids and adults struggling with depression?

» How can our faith in Jesus help us with depression?

Family Fun

Crank up the praise music and have a dance party in the living room or outside if the weather is nice. Fresh air, sunshine, exercise, and worshipping Jesus are an unbeatable combination for bringing hope and joy in the midst of despair. Just a few minutes of fun together can lighten the load and refresh the soul. Be silly and laugh as much as possible. Afterward, find a funny movie and cuddle for family movie night. There's truth to the adage, "Laughter is the best medicine," so be sure to laugh out loud as often as possible!

Baking Buddies

Life is filled with hard things and the weight of it can often feel overwhelming, but God promises us hope in the midst of the heaviness. Psalm 42:5 says, "*Why am I discouraged? Why is my heart so sad? I will put my hope in God! I will praise him again—my Savior and my God!*" My prayer for you can be found in Romans 15:13: "*I pray that God, the source of hope, will fill you completely with joy and peace because you trust in him. Then you will overflow with confident hope through the power of the Holy Spirit.*" Today we are making Heavy Yet Hopeful Chocolate Cake to remind us that even when life feels really heavy, we can rest in the hope we have in Jesus Christ.

HEAVY YET HOPEFUL
CHOCOLATE CAKE

Ingredients

1 cup unsalted butter, softened
2 cups granulated sugar
1 ½ tsp. pure vanilla extract
3 large eggs
2 ½ cups flour
1 cup baking cocoa, sifted
2 tsp. baking soda
½ tsp. salt
½ cup instant chocolate pudding mix (small box 3.5 oz.)
2 ¼ cup buttermilk or milk of choice
1 cup semisweet chocolate chips

Icing

¼ cup water
¼ cup unsalted butter
½ tsp. vanilla extract
½ cup baking cocoa, sifted
1 ¾ cups powdered sugar, sifted
1-2 tbsp. heavy cream

Directions

Cake

Preheat oven to 350°F.

In bowl of stand mixer, or in large bowl with electric hand mixer, cream sugar, butter, and vanilla together.

Beat in eggs one at a time.

Add flour, cocoa, baking soda, salt, pudding mix, and buttermilk. Beat to combine.

Stir in chocolate chips.

Grease a Bundt cake pan and pour batter into prepared pan.

Bake for 30 minutes, then reduce temperature of oven to 325°F and bake for an additional 30-40 minutes, until a toothpick comes out clean with just a few crumbs.

Allow cake to cool completely before icing.

Use a large plate/platter, or cake stand and invert cake out of pan onto platter.

Icing

Heat water, butter, and vanilla in a medium sauce pan over medium heat until melted.

Remove from heat and stir in sifted cocoa.

Add sifted powdered sugar and 1 tablespoon of heavy cream. Stir together and add a little more heavy cream if needed to reach desired consistency. Icing should be thick but pourable.

Pour icing along the inside edge of the cake, then spread it over the top and sides. The icing will harden as it cools.

Serve and enjoy.

SECTION TWO

BEHAVIORAL CHALLENGES

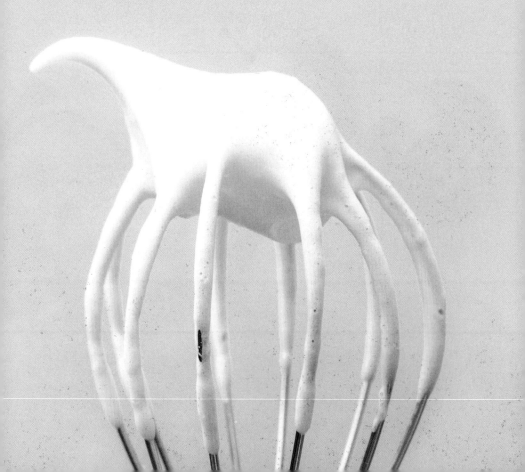

10

RESISTANCE TO SCHOOLWORK

*Someone who does careless work is as bad as
someone who destroys things.*
—Proverbs 18:9 (ERV)

Ugh. As I sipped my coffee, breathing in the final moments of blissful silence before the kids awoke for the day, I mentally prepared myself for the battle ahead. I'm not sure how it happened, but suddenly, every day, my kids had begun fighting me on schoolwork. The dream of homeschooling had turned into more of a nightmare. They would complain, saying things like, "It's too hard," "I don't want to do this today," and "Do we have to? I hate math!"

Somewhere along the way, we had fallen into a rut of complaining and resisting. Every. Single. Day. It was exhausting and frustrating for all of us. We needed a reset. So, one day, we paused. I talked with each child, separately, about what they were struggling with. We discussed ways to adjust our schedule to create a routine we all enjoyed more. We also talked about how much the privilege of homeschooling had blessed our family and how life would be vastly different for us in a traditional school setting.

I'd love to tell you that one conversation solved all our problems, but it didn't. However, I no longer found myself daily preparing for a battle. This in itself was a win! Thankfully, the following year, we changed the curriculum to something that included more reading out loud and subjects we could do together. We infused more movement and activities into our days. We reinforced the importance of being responsible and emphasized how it leads to more privileges and provides us with the internal reward of feeling proud of ourselves and what we accomplished.

Fast forward to today. My kids not only complete their schoolwork without complaining (at least most of the time), but they also do their daily chores like dishes, trash, and laundry without a fight. Bedrooms are still a fight, but I've learned to choose my battles wisely and not sweat the small stuff.

Parents' Prayer

Father, forgive me for times when I've resisted things You asked of me. Help me be patient with my kids and model responsibility for them. Give me creative strategies for structuring our homeschool or home life and reveal areas that need adjustment in order for my kids to thrive. In Jesus's name. Amen.

Teachable Moment

Psalm 128:2 teaches us that, "*You will enjoy the fruit of your labor. How joyful and prosperous you will be!*" If you could do anything in life, what would you want to do? What are some skills you need in order to accomplish your goal? The schoolwork you do today helps prepare you to fulfill your dreams tomorrow. We learn in Galatians 6:7 (NKJV), "*Do not be deceived, God is not mocked; for whatever a man sows, that he will also reap.*" If you plant brussels sprouts, don't expect to grow a watermelon. If you work hard, you produce good fruit. Skills and responsibility you learn today will help you succeed in the future.

Together, we're going to write a new daily plan to create realistic goals for your child's schoolwork and household tasks. Discuss the benefits of following through, such as internal rewards like how it feels good to complete tasks, and external rewards like screen time afterward and playing with friends. Explore and evaluate what you're currently doing and seek feedback from your child. What do they enjoy or not enjoy—and why? How would they like to do it differently? Also lay out the consequences for not completing the tasks. Then be sure to follow through. It takes consistency and commitment to build better habits.[2]

Conversation Connection

  » What does it mean to be responsible?

  » What are some of your responsibilities as a kid?

  » What are some of my responsibilities as an adult and parent?

  » What would happen if everyone stopped acting responsibly?

  » How can we work together to make school and work more fun?

Family Fun

Grab a rope or roll up a sheet to make a long rope and play a game of tug-of-war. Mark a line in the middle. Whoever pulls the other person or team across that line wins. Explain that when your child resists schoolwork, it feels like you are in an endless game of tug-of-war and that's exhausting. When you're tired from tug-of-war with them over schoolwork, you have less energy to be the fun parent you want to be and do the activities they like to do.

---

2. For additional ideas on homeschooling, download my free *Guide to Surviving Seriously Stressful Homeschool Days* at katiejtrent.com/strategies-for-surviving-stressful-homeschool-days.

Explain how people can do anything when they work together because tasks can be divided or shared. Then create a bucket list of things you and your kids can do together when they finish their schoolwork without the tug-of-war. This can include things like cuddling and reading a book aloud together, movies, games, outings, and playing together. Finally, when they don't resist schoolwork, reward their efforts with one of the activities and praise them profusely.

Baking Buddies

When you constantly resist your work, you find yourself in an endless game of tug-of-war in which everyone loses. It pulls your family apart and doesn't honor God. Psalm 34:14 says, *"Turn away from evil and do good. Search for peace, and work to maintain it."* Today we're making Tug-of-War Apple Pull-Apart Bread to help us remember how much our behavior impacts those around us.

TUG-OF-WAR APPLE PULL-APART BREAD

Ingredients

1 can refrigerated biscuits (honey butter ones or some other type)
3 apples, finely diced
1 tsp. lemon juice
⅓ cup brown sugar
2 tbsp. granulated sugar
½ tsp. vanilla extract
1 tsp. cinnamon
¼ tsp. ground ginger
½ tsp. ground nutmeg
¼ tsp. ground allspice
1 tbsp. cornstarch

Glaze

1 tsp. vanilla extract
¾ cup powdered sugar
1 tbsp. half-and-half (can substitute milk or milk alternative)

Directions

Grease a 9x5" loaf pan and set it aside.

Peel and finely dice the apples (throw away the cores).

In a skillet over medium heat, cook diced apples, lemon juice, sugars, spices, and cornstarch for several minutes, until thickened. Stir constantly so it doesn't burn. Then, set it aside to cool.

Preheat oven to 350°F.

Spread flour onto your surface and remove the biscuits from the package, leaving them together in the cylinder shape. Flatten and roll biscuits out into rectangle with a rolling pin.

Spread the cooled apple mixture evenly over the biscuits and cut into pieces by slicing lengthwise down the middle and then into 1" strips.

Tilt your pan on its side for easy layering. Stack the chunks of biscuit with the filling facing upward into your tilted pan. Layer one from the left side then one from the right side, stacking until they reach the other end of the pan.

Bake for 40-50 minutes or until it is golden brown.

Remove from pan to allow to cool on wire rack.

In a medium bowl, whisk together vanilla extract, powdered sugar, and half-and-half for the glaze.

Place loaf on serving tray and pour glaze over top. Allow it to set for a few minutes. Then serve warm or enjoy later.

11

PERFECTIONISM

Each time he said, "My grace is all you need.
My power works best in weakness." So now I am glad to boast about
my weaknesses, so that the power of Christ can work through me.
That's why I take pleasure in my weaknesses, and in the insults,
hardships, persecutions, and troubles that I suffer for Christ.
For when I am weak, then I am strong.
—2 Corinthians 12:9–10

I struggled with perfectionism throughout my life, so it shouldn't have come as such a surprise to me when my daughter battled it too—but it did. I thought because I homeschooled her, encouraged her unconditionally, and didn't grade her that she wouldn't battle with perfectionism as I had. Apparently, it's not necessarily a learned behavior, but an innate desire to succeed that drives our children to strive for perfection.

It began with wanting to get her letters perfect early on in homeschool. Kendra would erase and erase, no matter how many times I assured her it was okay to leave it how she wrote it the first time. Then she began pushing me to give her letter grades on her schoolwork. I'm still not sure where she discovered the grading system.

Perfectionism most often manifests in Kendra's art these days. She has a vision in her head of what she wants and becomes distraught when it doesn't work out exactly the same way. I've watched helplessly from the sidelines as she's thrown away completed art projects or partially finished ones that didn't turn out perfectly. She also tends to get upset if she doesn't master a new skill immediately.

Perfectionism immobilizes us with the fear of failure to the point where we may refuse to start something if we aren't confident of our eventual success. Breaking free from the bonds of perfectionism requires an understanding that such an ideal is an illusion meant to imprison us. We are perfectly imperfect people desperately in need of a Savior.

Parents' Prayer

Awesome God, forgive me for striving for perfection when only Your Son Jesus is perfect. Free my children from the bonds of perfectionism that hinder them and help them to experience Your grace in all of their imperfections. In Jesus's name I pray. Amen.

Teachable Moment

Matthew 5:48 says, "*But you are to be perfect, even as your Father in heaven is perfect.*" However, the Greek word translated as "perfect" is *teleios*, which means "complete in all its parts, full grown."[3] We are to grow more like Christ each day, but God doesn't expect perfection. We have only to look at the people He highlights in the Bible to understand that in admitting our imperfections, God is able to shine through our brokenness and light up this world.

Ask, "Can you think of some imperfect people God chose over more perfect people?" (For example, David's own father didn't think he could possibly become a king, so he presented his other sons to the prophet Samuel first; Esther was an orphan who became queen; Moses was a discarded child who killed a man, ran away in fear, and couldn't speak well,

---

3. 5046. teleios. *Strong's Greek Concordance.*

but God chose him to lead the Israelites out of captivity in Egypt; and the apostle Paul, who wrote two-thirds of the New Testament, persecuted Christians when he was known as Saul, but God used him in powerful ways.)

For today's lesson, at the sink or outside, you will need a paper or foam cup and something for poking a hole. I also recommend some yellow food dye as it makes the water easier to see. Tell your child, "The cup is perfect, without flaw, so whatever you fill it with stays inside." Fill the cup three-quarters full with water and stir in a few drops of dye.

Ask, "Does this cup need anything from you to hold the water in?" (No.) "God has created us to be His temples, carriers of His light in this world. But when we try to be perfect, none of His light pours out onto others. However, when we allow our flaws to be seen, God gets the glory, instead of us. Watch what happens when I poke a tiny hole in the cup. What will happen if I poke a lot of holes in it? The more we admit our weaknesses, the more God can be glorified and shine through us." Paul explains this in 2 Corinthians 12:9–10, the Scripture for today. Let's pray and ask God to help us appreciate our imperfections:

Dear God, thank You for sending Your perfect Son Jesus to die for my sins. I admit that I need a Savior and ask for forgiveness for my sins. Help me stop striving for perfection and let Your light shine through me onto others. In Jesus's name I pray. Amen.

For another fun activity, get a sheet of black construction paper and write the name "Jesus" in white crayon or chalk. Have your kids use a toothpick to poke out holes in His name. Then write "Jesus" on another piece of black paper without holes. Go into a dark room or closet and shine a flashlight directly behind the paper without holes while your child stands in front of it. Then do it again with the other paper. Explain that our flaws, like the holes, allow Jesus's light to shine through us onto others.

Conversation Connection

- » What does perfection mean?

- » What do you fear might happen if you aren't perfect in something?

- » What does imperfection mean?

- » Why would someone want to celebrate their imperfections?

- » Who are some examples of imperfect people God has used in extraordinary ways?

Family Fun

Grab a bag for everyone and go on a treasure hunt around the house for five or ten minutes to collect as many imperfect objects as each of you can find. Come back together and take turns sharing your bounty. Talk about how the imperfections turn ordinary items into extraordinary treasures. If you're feeling crafty, you can also create mosaic images to imitate stained glass and talk about how all the broken pieces of our lives work together to bring beauty and glory to God's name. Romans 8:28 promises: *"And we know that God causes everything to work together for the good of those who love God and are called according to his purpose for them."*

Baking Buddies

God created us perfectly imperfect. Ecclesiastes 7:20 says, *"Not a single person on earth is always good and never sins."* When we embrace our imperfections, God gets the glory, and we become vessels for His use. We're going to make Perfectly Imperfect Piñata Cupcakes today to remind us that the holes or imperfections in our lives allow God's light to shine through. We can learn to find joy in the messy middle of life.

PERFECTLY IMPERFECT PIÑATA CUPCAKES

For easy cupcakes, make the box cake mix of your choice with the canned frosting of your choice. Once the cupcakes cool, cut a circle in the middle of the cupcake and use a spoon to dig out a hole (don't go all the way to the bottom). Pour in your favorite candies or sprinkles to the top of the cupcake. Then frost. Or you can use the recipe below to make chocolate cupcakes from scratch.

Ingredients

2 cups heavy cream
1 lb. dark chocolate pieces
1 cup dark cocoa powder
2 cups boiling water
1 cup butter, softened
2 ¼ cups granulated sugar
4 large eggs
1 tbsp. vanilla
2 ¾ cups all-purpose flour
2 tsp. baking soda
½ tsp. baking powder
½ tsp. salt
1½ cups candy coated chocolates or other small candies or sprinkles
You'll want either a piping bag with a piping tip, or a plastic bag to use as a piping bag (cut a small hole in one of the bottom corners to squeeze out the frosting) or you can simply spread the ganache frosting on top with a butter knife.

Directions

Preheat oven to 350°F and prepare 30 cupcake liners in cupcake pans.

In a small pot, pour cream and bring to simmer over medium heat.

Place chocolate chunks in a medium bowl. Carefully pour hot cream over chocolate. Wait 10 minutes, then whisk until smooth. Set aside for an hour to allow to cool and set up. (*This will become your frosting.*)

In another medium bowl, whisk together cocoa powder and boiling water until smooth. Set aside to cool.

In the bowl of your stand mixer (or another large bowl with electric hand mixer), cream butter and sugar together until creamy.

Add eggs one at a time and beat until fluffy. Add vanilla and mix until combined.

In a separate bowl, combine flour, baking soda, baking powder, and salt. Whisk to combine.

Add dry ingredients to batter along with the cooled cocoa mixture and mix until well combined.

Scoop batter into cupcake liners (fill approximately ¾ full).

Bake on middle rack for approximately 15 minutes (may need to make in two batches).

Allow cupcakes to cool for approximately 30 minutes.

Use a paring knife to cut a circle out of the top middle of cupcake and use a small spoon to dig out the center of the cupcakes. (You can set these crumbs aside in a bowl to eat or mix with a scoop of frosting and make cake balls.)

Fill the cupcake holes with assorted candies or sprinkles to the tops.

Place cooled ganache frosting into piping bag with tip of choice and pipe it over the tops. Feel free to decorate with additional sprinkles or candies.

12

TATTLING

Believers, do not speak against or slander one another.
He who speaks [self-righteously] against a brother or judges his brother
[hypocritically], speaks against the Law and judges the Law. If you
judge the Law, you are not a doer of the Law but a judge of it.
—James 4:11 (AMP)

Oh, the *endless* tattling. I didn't know it was possible to find so many things to tattle on each other about. But I've learned the possibilities are limitless, especially in high-stress times. During seasons of transition, my kiddos struggled a lot with this behavior. Maybe you've been there too. We had already tried the whole, "Only tell us if it's something *major*, like someone's bleeding, dying, or doing something extremely unsafe."

Well, wouldn't you know those sweet little darlings' definitions of *major* is *everything*— *all the time!* It sounds like this:

» "He looked at me funny."

» "She said *sorry* in a mean voice."

» "He won't play how I want him to."

» "She's bossing me around."

I could go on...and on...but for all of our sakes, I'll leave it there. Because I know, sweet mama, that you probably have plenty of tattling stories too.

I often wondered why all kids seem to know to tattle from the time they are toddlers. As much as I hated to admit it, I realized it is a God-given trait—an innate desire for justice and righteousness trapped in the heart of an underdeveloped brain and immature spirit. As parents, we get to wrestle with how to tame the tattling beast without stripping our kids of their desire to fight for what is right. No pressure, huh?

Young children think very concretely and have great difficulty with abstract concepts. Things are right or wrong. Black or white. They struggle to apply reason and logic in complex situations because their brains haven't fully developed yet. So, when someone says a bad word, is mean to them, or breaks a rule, they compulsively run to the safety of their parents to set the world right again.

Thankfully, with much effort and repetition, we can give our kids the tools to solve problems and resolve conflicts as they arise. We can encourage the heart behind it—at least when it's justice and not retribution. For the Bible warns: *"Don't seek revenge or carry a grudge against any of your people. Love your neighbor as yourself. I am God"* (Leviticus 19:18 MSG).

Parents' Prayer

Jesus, help me not to seek revenge or hold a grudge when I am wronged and to teach my children to do the same. Purify our hearts and fill us with Your love and compassion for one another. Equip us to be problem-solvers and peacemakers. In Jesus's name we pray. Amen.

Teachable Moment

Tattling is when you try to get someone in trouble for little things that you could solve on your own. James 4:11 (ERV) says, *"Brothers and sisters, don't say anything against each other. If you criticize your brother or sister in Christ or judge them, you are criticizing and judging the law they follow. And when you are judging the law, you are not a follower of the law. You have become a judge."*

We want to learn how to resolve our conflicts with each other instead of trying to get them in trouble. In the Gospel of Matthew, Jesus teaches us how to handle conflict:

If a fellow believer hurts you, go and tell him—work it out between the two of you. If he listens, you've made a friend. If he won't listen, take one or two others along so that the presence of witnesses will keep things honest, and try again. If he still won't listen, tell the church. If he won't listen to the church, you'll have to start over from scratch, confront him with the need for repentance, and offer again God's forgiving love.

(Matthew 18:15–17 MSG)

Let your kids know:

It's important to calm yourself first so you are thinking clearly. If it's a minor issue, ask yourself if it's better to just let it go. Otherwise, you want to work on solving the problem with that person. Only after you're calm and have been unable to resolve the problem together would you come involve me or another adult. Sometimes people may try to convince you to keep a secret about something bad by saying it would be tattling. But when a person does something that could harm someone or makes you feel unsafe, it is always important to share that with a parent or trusted adult.

Let's create a list of things that would be tattling and things that should always be told to an adult immediately. If your child can't read, you could create a poster with pictures they draw or images from the Internet to help them remember the behaviors you list.

Here are some questions for kids to ask themselves to figure out if something is tattling:

1. Am I or anyone else in danger because of this behavior?

2. Could something bad happen if I don't share this with an adult?

3. Can I resolve this on my own? (By ignoring them, walking away, or asking them to stop.)

4. Why do I want to tell on them? Do I want to hurt or punish them or am I honestly trying to help?

Conversation Connection

» Why do you tattle on someone? What do you want to happen when you tell an adult on them?

» If you chose not to tattle, what are some other things you could do in those times?

» How can you tell the difference between something that you should immediately tell an adult and tattling?

» What are some things we should always tell an adult about right away?

Family Fun

Explain to your kids before playing that the Bible says, "*A truly wise person uses few words; a person with understanding is even-tempered*" (Proverbs 17:27). When Moses faced a huge army of Egyptian soldiers about to overtake him and the Israelites before God parted the Red Sea,

God encouraged Moses, "*The* L*ORD* *will fight for you while you [only need to]* *keep silent and remain calm*" (Exodus 14:14 AMP). The same advice holds true for you. Most of the time when you are upset about something your sibling or friend has done, you need only to keep silent and remain calm.

The Lord fights for you. He is your defender. When you're calm, you're more likely to resolve the problem—even if the solution is to simply walk away and go play something by yourself for a bit. Today we're going to have some fun playing Pictionary, a silent game to remind us of God's advice.

You can utilize a large piece of paper, a dry-erase board, or head outside with chalk to play on your sidewalk. Take turns drawing silly items or situations and trying to guess what they are. You can also utilize this game time to address situations where tattling isn't necessary versus dangerous situations where you want your kids to immediately come tell you.

Baking Buddies

The Bible teaches us, "*If someone does you wrong, don't try to pay them* *back by hurting them. Try to do what everyone thinks is right. Do the best* *you can to live in peace with everyone*" (Romans 12:17–18 ERV). Today we're making Tattle-Free Chocolate Cookie Trifle to remind us not to trifle with tattling but instead to layer our lives with love and goodness.

TATTLE-FREE CHOCOLATE COOKIE TRIFLE

This recipe includes brownies. You can whip up your favorite boxed brownie mix or make them from scratch. You can even make them gluten-free. Simply make the boxed brownies as directed (you will likely need eggs, vegetable oil, and water along with mix) or use the recipe below to make them from scratch.

Brownies

10 tablespoons unsalted butter
1 ½ cups granulated sugar
¾ cup unsweetened cocoa powder
¼ teaspoon salt
1 tsp. vanilla extract
2 large eggs
½ cup all-purpose flour

Pudding

1 pkg. (3.4 oz.) instant cheesecake pudding mix
1 tsp. vanilla extract
14 oz. sweetened condensed milk
½ cup cold water
8 oz. frozen whipped topping, thawed

Trifle

8 oz. frozen whipped topping, thawed
12 chocolate sandwich cookies, crumbled
Large trifle bowl or glass serving dish (*or you can make individual trifles in mason jars or clear plastic disposable cups*)

Directions

Brownies: Prepare as instructed on box, or if making from this recipe, preheat oven to 325°F. Line an 8x8" square cake pan with parchment paper (allow the paper to hang over two sides for easy removal).

In a small saucepan over medium-low heat, combine butter, sugar, salt, and cocoa powder. Whisk continuously until sugar dissolves into the butter. If working with young children, you can place mixture in a microwave-safe bowl and microwave in 20-second increments, stirring each time until sugar is dissolved. It may still look a little gritty, but that's okay.

Remove from heat and allow mixture to cool for 3-5 minutes so it is warm but not hot.

Add the eggs and vanilla and stir to combine.

Pour in flour and beat with wooden spoon or spatula. Don't overmix. Stir just until flour is incorporated.

Spread batter evenly into your prepared pan.

Bake 20-30 minutes. The edges should be crisp, and the middle will look a little gooey. A toothpick inserted into the middle should come out with a few wet crumbs but not liquid batter. Allow brownies to cool completely before removing from the pan to make your trifle.

You can make the brownies the day before or same day.

Pudding: In a large bowl, combine pudding mix, sweetened condensed milk, vanilla, and water. Mix until smooth. Fold in 8 oz. whipped topping until blended.

Trifle: Cut cooled brownies into 1" squares. In trifle bowl, layer half the brownies. Add half the pudding, then 4 oz. of the remaining whipped topping. Repeat layers. Finally, garnish with crumbled cookies. Refrigerate for at least two hours before serving.

If making individual trifles, kids can make their own by adding a brownie, then a dollop of pudding followed by whipped topping, and topping with crumbled cookies.

13

UNFORGIVENESS

Make allowance for each other's faults,
and forgive anyone who offends you. Remember, the Lord forgave
you, so you must forgive others.
—Colossians 3:13

Betrayed. Rejected. Abused. Slandered. Mocked…I could continue, but I know you get the point. And I imagine you've experienced some, if not all, of these painful scenarios. I certainly have. But the Bible leads me to believe that I'm not alone in my experiences, and more than that, God never leaves me alone in my pain.

Forgiveness is probably one of the most difficult things God asks of us. Yet I believe our struggle with forgiveness gives us a glimpse into the magnitude of our own transgressions—and Christ's sacrifice for us on the cross. It can help put into perspective the truth that the suffering we experience as we wrestle with unforgiveness is nothing compared to the sufferings of Christ to atone for our sins and restore us eternally with God—despite how painful it may feel at the time.

As difficult as this concept is for us to grasp, it's even more challenging for our children, whose brains and executive functions are still developing. How can we just forgive someone who has hurt us so deeply? Someone who isn't even sorry for what they've done or continues to hurt us again and again? Even adults wrestle with these challenging questions. But the Bible is clear on the matter. There is never an exception to this rule of forgiveness.

It's vital that we impress upon our children the importance of forgiveness. It's not optional, but a mandatory expectation from God. Jesus tells us:

If you forgive those who sin against you, your heavenly Father will forgive you. But if you refuse to forgive others, your Father will not forgive your sins. (Matthew 6:14–15)

Now, that doesn't mean it will be easy. Quite the opposite, in fact, and we need to help our kids understand this. Forgiveness is often an ongoing process—a daily battle against bitterness that builds as we withhold our compassion. But as we help our children learn that unforgiveness only imprisons and hurts us, not the person we're refusing to forgive, it allows them to realize the most powerful choice we can make in painful situations is to forgive. To release the hurt and not allow that person or the enemy to gain a foothold in our hearts or take up space in our minds. There is incredible freedom in forgiveness.

Parents' Prayer

God, forgive me for withholding forgiveness at times. Help me to forgive and release all those who've hurt me so I may model forgiveness for my children. Heal their hearts of the pain they're holding onto and give me the words to comfort and guide them on their journey of forgiveness so they may be free from the chains of unforgiveness. In Jesus's name I pray. Amen.

Teachable Moment

Imagine the person you're mad at. Now imagine that to punish or hurt that person back, you begin to hit yourself, and everything you do to try to punish the person who hurt you only ends up hurting you instead. That's what happens with unforgiveness. It doesn't destroy the other person, but it slowly hurts you as it hardens your heart.

Not only that, but the Bible teaches us that if we want God to forgive us, we need to forgive everyone who hurts us. It doesn't matter how many times a person hurts you; Jesus tells us to continually forgive them. He shares a parable (a story) of an unforgiving debtor in Matthew 18:21–35. (Depending on the age of your child, either summarize the story for them, or read it together. Talk about how that applies to their situation of withholding forgiveness from someone.)

Jesus tells us we must even go beyond forgiveness; we should actually love the person who hurt us.

Our Scriptures tell us that if you see your enemy hungry, go buy that person lunch, or if he's thirsty, get him a drink. Your generosity will surprise him with goodness. Don't let evil get the best of you; get the best of evil by doing good. (Romans 12:20–21 MSG)

This may also be a good place to talk about healthy boundaries. Forgiveness doesn't mean we keep putting ourselves in unsafe situations. We can forgive those who've abused us, but we don't have to remain in relationship with them.

It often helps to write out our feelings. Write a letter (or for younger kids, draw a picture) expressing what happened and why you're having trouble forgiving. At the end of the letter or picture, write (or say), "I choose to forgive _____ for _____." And write out a prayer of blessing over them. It could be as simple as, "Jesus, I choose to forgive my sister for hurting my feelings. Heal my heart and bless her in every area of her life. Amen." Encourage your child to pray that prayer again any time they start to feel upset about the situation.

Conversation Connection

> » Why is it so hard to forgive sometimes?

> » What can you do when you're having trouble forgiving someone?

> » Why is it important to forgive?

> » How many times does the Bible say we have to forgive someone?

Family Fun

Play a game of Forgiving Freeze Tag. One person is "it" and chases the other players. Once a player is tagged, they are frozen in place until they say, "I choose to forgive _____ for _____." The other players scatter and the person who has been tagged becomes the tagger after they have chosen to forgive. *Explain that unforgiveness causes us to get stuck in our hurts and only forgiveness can set us free.*

Baking Buddies

When we refuse to forgive others, we get frozen in unforgiveness. It hardens our hearts from the inside out and ends up affecting every area of our lives. Proverbs 28:14 (MSG) says, "*A tenderhearted person lives a blessed life; a hardhearted person lives a hard life.*" Today, we're going to make some Frozen Forgiveness Fruit Crumble to remind us not to allow unforgiveness to harden our hearts and hurt our lives.

FROZEN FORGIVENESS FRUIT CRUMBLE (GLUTEN-FREE)

Ingredients

Berry Filling

4 cups frozen mixed berries (don't thaw ahead of time)
3 tbsp. granulated sugar
3 tbsp. gluten-free 1:1 baking flour
1 tsp. lemon zest
Pinch of salt

Crumble Topping

1 cup old fashioned rolled oats (gluten-free)
½ cup brown sugar
6 tbsp. gluten-free 1:1 baking flour
½ cup butter (cut into small cubes)

Directions

Preheat oven to 350°F.

In a medium bowl, combine berries, sugar, 3 tbsp. flour, lemon zest and salt. Toss to combine and set aside.

In a separate bowl, combine oats, brown sugar, 6 tbsp. flour, and cubes of butter. Use a fork to combine into small crumbles and set aside.

Pour berry mix into 8x8" baking pan. Top with crumble and spread evenly.

Bake uncovered for 45-60 minutes, until filling is bubbly and top is golden.

Allow to cool 30-60 minutes before serving. Top with whipped cream or ice cream if desired.

14

MODESTY/PURITY

Don't you realize that your body is the temple of the Holy Spirit,
who lives in you and was given to you by God?
You do not belong to yourself, for God bought you with a high price.
So you must honor God with your body.
—1 Corinthians 6:19–20

From the time our kids were babies, we were conscientious about the way we dressed them. I'll never forget shopping for our baby's first swimsuit and being appalled at the string bikinis for babies! Babies! We live in an overly sexualized world, and we have to be diligent about protecting our kids. It's no wonder elementary-aged children are addicted to pornography, and we're experiencing a human trafficking epidemic! From shopping malls to kids' television programming to a stroll down the street, our children's innocent eyes are constantly assaulted.

We've got to teach our kids how to guard their hearts and protect their eyes as they stand for purity in a sexually corrupt and distorted world. We must teach our children that our bodies are a temple of the Holy Spirit, and we want to honor and protect our bodies. There are a lot of great resources out there that dive deeper into various areas related to purity—how to protect your children against sexual abuse, pornography, and other dangers, depending on your children's ages. But for the purpose of this chapter, we're simply going to focus on teaching our kids to honor their bodies and dress appropriately as they guard their eyes and ears from impure things.

When my daughter turned nine, she became infatuated with the idea of *crop tops*. She'd seen her homeschool friends wearing them at the park, young girls wearing them on various TV shows, and store racks filled with these belly-baring shirts. When Kendra asked if she'd ever be able to wear one, I wanted to understand why she was drawn to them. This is critical when approaching our children about a struggle. By understanding the reason behind it, we are better equipped to explore and address the issue instead of just panicking and shutting them down.

Kendra has always been a creative dresser. It's one of the many ways she likes to artistically express herself. So, when she wanted to wear a crop top, we explored ideas for expressing herself with clothes in a way that honored her body and God.

With our son, we've talked to Jordan about guarding and averting his eyes because he's bombarded with images of girls and women in scantily clad clothing while we are out and about.

We also talk with our kids about their bodies, private parts, healthy boundaries, and privacy. I wish I could say this is a challenge that requires only a single conversation, but the truth is, it needs to be an ongoing and ever evolving conversation as our children grow older. We must diligently guard and protect our kids from the sexual immorality around us. And we can't do it alone! We need the Holy Spirit's help each and every day. Pray for wisdom and allow God to lead you as you make daily decisions and cultivate conversations about modesty and purity. (See James 1:5.)

Parents' Prayer

Holy Spirit, increase my wisdom and discernment. Teach me to guard and protect my children's hearts and minds from the lusts of the flesh. Help us to honor our bodies as Your living temples. In Jesus's name I pray. Amen.

Teachable Moment

Share today's Scripture reading (1 Corinthians 6:19–20). What was the high price that God paid for us? (Jesus dying on the cross for us.) What are some ways we can honor God with our body? Let's create a list. (This could include eating healthy foods, exercising, getting enough sleep, dressing modestly, listening to Christian music, and being careful about what shows we watch, the conversations we listen to, the words we say, and the thoughts we think.)

We also need to protect our eyes and ears. Psalm 101:3 (ERV) says, "I will not even look at anything shameful. I hate all wrongdoing. I want no part of it!" Things that are "shameful" can include images in magazines or on billboards, commercials, movies, or video games—anything that doesn't honor God. In our world today, sin is everywhere, and we must actively guard against it. Proverbs 4:25–27 tells us: "Look straight ahead, and fix your eyes on what lies before you. Mark out a straight path for your feet; stay on the safe path. Don't get sidetracked; keep your feet from following evil." Much of what the world today calls good is actually evil, which is why we need to choose our friends carefully and be mindful of what we expose ourselves to.

If your kids are older and you want to discuss physical intimacy, 2 Timothy 2:22 is a good Scripture to begin this conversation. Then, you could talk about God's design for marriage. (See Genesis 2:24; 1 Corinthians 6:18; 1 Thessalonians 4:3–5; Hebrews 13:4.)

Conversation Connection

» What does the Bible mean when it says our bodies are living temples of the Holy Spirit?

» How can we honor God with our bodies?

» What are some ways we might be dishonoring God with our bodies?

» What should we do if we see something immodest or impure?

Family Fun

Play the Diligently Dodge Danger Game—otherwise known as dodge ball. Grab a few soft foam or rubber balls and talk about how we need to be on guard for dangerous situations in order to keep our hearts and minds pure. Team up or play free-for-all. Try to dodge the balls being thrown your way. If you don't have balls to use, you can wad up pieces of paper to throw. You could also have a nerf gun battle and talk about how the world is warring for our souls, so we need to fight to remain pure.

Baking Buddies

Today we're making Pure Goodness Granola Parfaits to help us remember to keep our hearts, minds, and bodies pure so we can be vessels worthy for God. Grab a dirty cup and a clean one and ask your kids which one they would prefer to build their parfait in. Share this Scripture:

If you keep yourself pure, you will be a special utensil for honorable use. Your life will be clean, and you will be ready for the Master to use you for every good work. Run from anything that stimulates youthful lusts. Instead, pursue righteous living, faithfulness, love, and peace. Enjoy the companionship of those who call on the Lord with pure hearts.
(2 Timothy 2:21–22)

Just as we wouldn't want to build our parfaits in dirty glasses, we want to keep our hearts, minds, and bodies pure because we are temples for the Holy Spirit.

PURE GOODNESS
GRANOLA PARFAITS

If you want to enjoy this for breakfast, make the granola the night before and store in an airtight container. It also makes a great afternoon snack.

Ingredients

4 cups old-fashioned rolled oats (use gluten-free if needed)

1 ½ cups raw nuts and/or seeds; use a mix of whatever you like (I love almonds, cashews, pecans, chia seeds, flax seeds, and pumpkin seeds)

1 tsp. kosher salt (use ½ tsp. if you're including a lot of salted nuts)

½ tsp. ground cinnamon

½ cup coconut oil or olive oil

¾ cup honey (or maple syrup)

2 tsp. vanilla extract

⅔ cup dried fruit (raisins, dried cranberries, bananas, mangos, apples, etc.)

*You could also top with ½ cup of extras if you want (mini chocolate chips, coconut flakes, etc.)

2 cups vanilla Greek yogurt (can also use another flavor if preferred)

1-2 cups fruit of choice (berries, diced apples, sliced bananas, mangos, pears, peaches, etc.)

Directions

Preheat oven to 350°F. Line half-sheet pan (rimmed) with parchment paper.

In a large bowl, mix oats, nuts/seeds, salt, and cinnamon. (*Do not include fruit yet*)

In a small bowl, mix oil, honey, and vanilla, then pour it over the oat mixture and stir until everything is lightly coated.

Spread mixture evenly into prepared sheet pan.

Bake for 10 minutes, then gently stir and press down with your spatula (this helps make it clumpier). Bake an additional 10-15 minutes. Remove from oven to finish crisping. (Don't overbake. It should be lightly golden).

Allow granola to cool completely (approximately 45-60 minutes), then top with dried fruit. Use your hands to break it into chunks or stir with a spoon for smaller chunks.

In small bowls or cups, layer a scoop of yogurt, granola, fruit, then lightly drizzle with honey and repeat the layers. Serve and enjoy!

15

LAZINESS

Work willingly at whatever you do, as though you were
working for the Lord rather than for people.
Remember that the Lord will give you an inheritance as your reward,
and that the Master you are serving is Christ.
—Colossians 3:23–24

It's easy to fall into a trap of laziness. We live in a wearying world. Did you know it's possible to be busy and lazy at the same time? We often keep ourselves occupied doing some things while neglecting the most important. I'm certainly guilty of this. Laziness is idleness or an unwillingness to work at something or utilize your energy for it.

Our kids can fall into this trap too. They can get so wrapped up in themselves and their own desires that they become lazy. Perhaps your child refuses to help around the house, complete their schoolwork, or engage in physical activities. If we aren't careful, laziness becomes a habit that's hard to break.

Paul wrote:

When we were with you, we gave you this rule: "Whoever will not work should not be allowed to eat." We hear that some people in your group refuse to work. They are doing nothing except being busy in the lives of others. Our instruction to them is to stop bothering others, to start working and earn their own food. It is by the authority of the Lord Jesus Christ that we are urging them to do this. Brothers and sisters, never get tired of doing good. (2 Thessalonians 3:10–13 ERV)

In our family, we emphasize the importance of working together. Whether it's maintaining our home, serving our community, tackling projects, or taking care of each other; we're constantly teaching our children that we all have a part to play. We don't pay our kids to complete household chores because we want them to recognize that part of the responsibility of owning a home is maintaining it. In order for us to enjoy time together as a family, we all need to help out.

When our kids struggle with laziness, we want to explore the root cause. Maybe they've simply developed a bad habit they need to break. Perhaps they're feeling overwhelmed with some aspect of life and need support to manage their emotions or expectations. They might be lacking proper motivation or the ability to address the issue.

Honest conversation, realistic expectations, natural consequences, and prayer can go a long way to instill good work habits in our homes.

Parents' Prayer

God, forgive me for my laziness. Help me and my children to work diligently as if working directly for You each day. Give me wisdom to know how to motivate and encourage my child to break free from laziness. In Jesus's name I pray. Amen.

Teachable Moment

The Bible warns us, *"Lazy people want much but get little, but those who work hard will prosper"* (Proverbs 13:4). Laziness means an unwillingness to work or being idle. You may not think it's a big deal, but the Bible teaches us, *"A lazy person is as bad as someone who destroys things"* (Proverbs 18:9). Do you know what all the great men and women in history have in common? (None of them were lazy!) They all worked hard and pursued their passions.

Study the life of an ant together. Ask your children what they already know about ants and make a list. Then study them. You can find information online or pick up a book from the library. I also encourage you to step outside, look for ants, and then sit down for a few minutes to study and watch them. What do you notice about them? Try to find an idle ant standing around doing nothing. You can't! (Unless it's dead…which is a lesson in and of itself.)

After you've studied and discussed ants, read Proverbs 6:6–11 together:

Take a lesson from the ants, you lazybones. Learn from their ways and become wise! Though they have no prince or governor or ruler to make them work, they labor hard all summer, gathering food for the winter. But you, lazybones, how long will you sleep? When will you wake up? A little extra sleep, a little more slumber, a little folding of the hands to rest—then poverty will pounce on you like a bandit; scarcity will attack you like an armed robber.

One of the best ways to break free from laziness is to set realistic goals. Talk about the issue your child is struggling with and set specific, measurable, realistic, and time-specific goals to help them break free from laziness and cultivate a habit of diligence. For younger kids, sticker charts work great to reinforce hard work and task completion. Be sure to celebrate and reward progress and talk about the benefits of their new habits. (How do they feel? What's different or better?)

Conversation Connection

 » What does it mean to be lazy?

» Why do you think it can hard to motivate yourself to do something?

» How can you break free from laziness?

» What's one thing you plan to be more productive with?

Family Fun

Time to play Lazy Lounging Llamas! Grab a large blanket, spread it out on the floor, and lie down on top of it. Have the kids take turns trying to pull you across the room on the blanket. You can rotate turns so everyone gets a chance to be in the blanket or do the pulling. Explain that when someone is lazy, they create more work for everyone else and become like a dead weight for others. Proverbs 12:24 tells us, "*Work hard and become a leader; be lazy and become a slave.*" Lazy llamas never lead. We want to fulfill all of God's plans for us, so must spend our time wisely and work diligently.

Baking Buddies

The Bible teaches us that "*those who work hard will prosper*" (Proverbs 13:4), and whatever we do, we should "*work as though [we] are working for the Lord*" (Colossians 3:23 ERV). Laziness puts a sour taste in people's mouths and sets us up for failure. Today we're making Lazy Lemon Sheet Cake to remind us not to lie around like a sheet in bed. We want to use our time wisely and honor God with our efforts and energy.

LAZY LEMON SHEET CAKE

Ingredients

1 cup (2 sticks) unsalted butter, softened
2 cups granulated sugar
4 large eggs
½ cup lemon juice
2 tbsp. lemon zest
½ tsp. lemon extract
1 tsp. vanilla extract
2 ½ cups all-purpose flour
1 tsp. baking soda
½ tsp. kosher salt
½ cup whole buttermilk

Frosting

8 oz. cream cheese, softened
½ cup unsalted butter, softened
1 tsp. lemon extract
2 ½ cups powdered sugar

Directions

Preheat oven to 350°F. Grease a 13x18" rimmed sheet cake pan with cooking spray.

In the bowl of a stand mixer (or large bowl), use the paddle attachment (or electric mixer) to cream butter, lemon zest, and sugar on medium speed for 2-4 minutes, until fluffy.

In a medium bowl, combine buttermilk, sour cream, eggs, lemon juice, vanilla, and lemon extract. Gently stir to combine.

In a medium bowl, whisk together flour, baking soda, and salt.

Gradually add flour mixture and wet mixture to your butter mixture. Alternate wet and dry until it's all incorporated, but don't overmix.

Pour batter into prepared pan and use a spatula to spread evenly.

Bake 20-25 minutes, or until a toothpick inserted into the center comes out with just a few crumbs. Allow to cool completely.

To make the frosting, beat the cream cheese and butter together in your stand mixer until creamy. Add in powdered sugar and lemon extract and mix until combined.

Spread frosting over cooled cake and enjoy. Be sure to cover cake with airtight lid so it doesn't dry out.

16

IMPULSIVITY

Careful planning leads to profit. Acting too quickly leads to poverty.
—Proverbs 21:5 (ERV)

Why'd you do that?!"

"You need to think before you act!!"

"Don't you know how dangerous that is?!"

Impulsivity is a frustrating trait that often leads us down a road of poor decisions. We've all acted impulsively or reacted without thinking at some point in our lives. In general, children are prone to impulsivity. As their brains develop, they learn how to think and reason before they act—but it takes practice and discipline to learn to control impulses.

For some children, impulsivity is difficult to manage. I've counseled hundreds of children who struggle with this problem. My husband James battles it too—and so do my kids. When a child battles impulsivity, it can feel like they're intentionally being disobedient, but that's often not the case.

Kendra used to struggle with impulsivity. She'd do things without thinking, making many decisions that drove James especially crazy. He would get so frustrated with her because he believed she was intentionally behaving badly. It took time for him to realize she truly couldn't help herself and was working hard to try to control her impulses.

One of the most important things I've learned in helping my child navigate the difficulties of impulsivity is to be patient and grace filled. As frustrating as their behaviors may be for us, they are even more frustrating for our kids. And children who have trouble with impulsivity often believe the lie that they're *bad* kids. They tend to get into trouble more frequently than others, and this can have a significant impact on their self-esteem.

To combat impulsive behavior, it helps to reinforce the times in which our child demonstrates self-control and thinks before acting. We want to highlight those moments and celebrate with them. We also want to let them know that our love and their worth aren't conditional.

It helps to remind ourselves that they aren't acting that way out of rebellion. It's simply an obstacle they have to learn to overcome. It's not easy, but with consistency, calm, and a bit of patience, they can learn to stop and think before they act.

Parents' Prayer

Jesus, help me be patient with my child as they learn to stop and think before they act. Give me wisdom on how to navigate this behavioral challenge with grace and patience. In Jesus's name I pray. Amen.

Teachable Moment

Impulsivity means acting without thinking, which often means doing things that hurt us and others. In order to overcome this, we need to learn to stop and think before we act. One impulsive action can undo years of hard work. We can see the truth of this in the life of Moses. In Exodus 2:11–15, Moses saw an Egyptian beating a fellow Hebrew man. After Moses quickly looked around to ensure no one was watching, he acted impulsively and killed the Egyptian. He didn't think through the consequences of his actions. Verses 14–15 tell us that not only was Moses seen, leading to animosity with his own people, but Pharaoh learned about the murder and tried to kill Moses. He fled for his life and ended up in Midian for many years.

Even after Moses encountered God and spent many years leading his people, Moses acted impulsively. In Numbers 20:8, God told Moses to speak over a rock so water could flow from it, but instead, Moses impulsively struck the rock with his staff. (See verse 11.) He was frustrated and acted without thinking. Verse 9 says, *"Moses did as he was told"* in gathering the people. He wasn't trying to rebel against God. He wasn't a bad man. In fact, Moses faithfully served the Lord for many years. Yet the consequences of one impulsive act caused Moses to miss out on the blessing of leading the people into the promised land.

Older kids can study additional men and women in the Bible who struggled with impulsivity and write about how their impulsive actions caused problems for them and others. They could also create a journal to track their own behaviors and decisions. For younger kids, the journal could simply be a picture of what happened and a smiley face or neutral face to indicate whether they stopped and thought before acting. You could also create a reward chart where they get to place a sticker every time they stop and think before acting, with an incentive when they reach the end of the chart. (A chart where they're tracking how many times they fail or losing points when they fall short will only lead to discouragement, so celebrate successes instead.)

Every action we take results in a consequence. We're going to work on stopping and thinking before we act so we can learn to weigh our choices before making a decision. Today we're going to make a stop light to remind us to stop and think before we act. And then we're going to practice using it.

Red Means Stop

Take deep breaths. Calm yourself down and take a break if you need to.

Yellow Means Think

Ask yourself: is it safe? Could it hurt me or someone else? What might happen if I do this? What choices do I have—and what is the best choice I can make?

Green Means Act

Do what you know is the right choice for you and others.

Conversation Connection

» Can you think of a time you acted without thinking? What happened?

» What could you have done instead? What might have happened if you made a different choice?

» Can you think of a time where you didn't act impulsively? Where you thought things through before acting? What happened?

» We learned about Moses and how his impulsivity hurt him. Can you think of anyone else in the Bible who acted impulsively? (For example, Esau sold his birthright for a meal in Genesis 25:32–33, and Peter cut off a man's ear in John 18:10.)

Family Fun

Play a game of Red Light-Green Light. You can play indoors, if necessary, though outdoors is best. Determine a starting line and a finish line. When you shout, "Green light," everyone moves quickly toward the finish line, but when you shout, "Red light," everyone has to immediately stop. Anyone who moves after "red light" must go back to the starting line.

After playing the traditional way, play the *stop and think* way. In this game, give a scenario, such as, "Your sister says something mean." Then say "stop" and have them practice taking deep breaths or counting backwards from ten to calm themselves down. When you say "think," have them raise their hands when they think of questions to ask themselves. They need to wait to be called on before answering (another impulse-control strategy), then share the question and answer. After everyone's had a turn, say "act" and have them act out their solution. Celebrate how well they practiced stopping and thinking before acting, and then try another scenario. Depending on their ages, they can even take turns being the one leading the game or coming up with a list of common scenarios.

Baking Buddies

The opposite of impulsive is deliberate. We want to be deliberate in our actions, so we stop and think before we act. We are encouraged to do this in Ephesians 5:15–17: "*So be careful how you live. Don't live like fools, but like those who are wise. Make the most of every opportunity in these evil days. **Don't act thoughtlessly**, but understand what the Lord wants you to do.*"

Today we're going to make Deliberate Dulce De Leche Donuts to help us remember to stop and think under pressure. When we make *dulce de leche* (sweet milk), we see that the contents of the can of sweetened condensed milk experience a lot of pressure and heat. By deliberately waiting out the heat, the contents are transformed. The same thing happens when we allow ourselves to be refined under pressure instead of trying to avoid the discomfort or immediately reacting to our situation without thinking. (If you want, after you boil the can, you can compare its contents to the contents of a regular can of sweetened condensed milk.) When we practice self-control and deliberately press through our struggles, we allow ourselves to be refined.

DELIBERATE DULCE DE LECHE DONUTS

Ingredients

1 can (14 oz.) sweetened condensed milk
1 package of mini biscuit dough
1 cup (2 sticks) butter or 4 cups of oil for frying
½ cup powdered sugar

Directions

Remove the label from the can of sweetened condensed milk. Place unopened can in the bottom of a large pot and fill with water until it covers the can by at least two inches.

Place pot over medium-high heat until it comes to a boil. Then reduce heat and allow water to simmer. Check the pot every 30 minutes or so to make sure the water remains at least 1" above the can (add more water as necessary).

Allow water to simmer for 2 ½ - 3 hours. Three hours will yield a darker, richer flavor.

An adult should carefully remove the can from the water with tongs (canning tongs work best if you have them). *It will be very hot.* Allow it to cool.

Once the can is cool enough, open it and dump contents into a bowl so you can whisk out any lumps.

Open the biscuit package (or feel free to make your own biscuits if you prefer). Press your thumb into the middle of the biscuit to create a small indent, then add a small scoop of dulce de leche into the center of the biscuit. Tuck the dough up over the filling and pinch the ends to seal it in and make a small ball. Continue until all of the biscuits have been filled, then set aside.

Heat a deep frying pan or Dutch oven on medium and place the sticks of butter or oil in the pan. Once the butter is melted, it's ready (or your oil needs to reach at least 350°F; I recommend using a candy thermometer to gauge the temperature).

Place a couple paper towels over a plate and set near the stove.

Fry the dough for approximately 3 minutes on each side (or until golden brown).

Carefully remove from pan using a slotted spoon or tongs and gently shake to remove excess oil before placing on paper towels.

Dust with powdered sugar and enjoy.

17

GOSSIPING

A gossip goes around telling secrets,
so don't hang around with chatterers.
—Proverbs 20:19

Throughout my life, I found myself on the outside of inner circles. I was invited but not valued—at least I didn't *feel* valued. I often ended up in the middle when my friends squabbled in middle school. One person in our group was mad at another and would share something with me, then the other person would. Even though I'd tell myself I was trying to be a good friend and a listening ear, it never ended well. At the time, I didn't understand how they both ended up mad at me, especially when I didn't share what they said about each other.

Over the years, however, I've learned that listening without correcting is still participating—it's coming into agreement with what was said. It's not enough to just not spread gossip. We have to actively address it and refuse to participate in the conversations. Speak up. Walk away. But don't stay and silently allow it to spread.

Gossip can be an incredibly difficult habit to break. Whether your child is the one who shares gossip or the one who listens to it without speaking up, it's a slippery slope. And if not corrected, gossip will follow us into our workplaces, families, and churches.

My husband and I started serving in ministry over fifteen years ago, and I've encountered *a lot* of gossip masquerading as ministry. I would be told, "Pray for so-and-so because..." or "I'm telling you this because I'm concerned about so-and-so." And honestly, I've fallen into the trap of gossiping too, whether sharing or listening. I can't tell you how many conversations I've walked away from beating myself up because of something I accidentally shared or stayed silent when I should've spoken up. But I've learned to be more mindful of what I share and how to set healthy boundaries when someone attempts to pull me into gossip. And those are skills I'm working diligently to teach my children.

Parents' Prayer

God, forgive me for gossiping or not speaking out against it when I hear it. Give me the words to say to help my children break free from gossip and grant them the courage to speak up when others attempt to pull them into gossip. In Jesus's name I pray. Amen.

Teachable Moment

The Bible warns us: "*And I tell you this, you must give an account on judgment day for every idle word you speak. The words you say will either acquit you or condemn you*" (Matthew 12:36–37). Gossip is as toxic as poison. The Bible cautions: "*Speak without thinking, and your words can cut like a knife. Be wise, and your words can heal*" (Proverbs 12:18 ERV).

Imagine a swimming pool polluted with poison. Your friend asks you to jump in with them. Would you do it? What about if you just had to stand in it, not swim in it? No. You still wouldn't want to. Gossip is the same way. Whether you're the one sharing the gossip or the one listening to it, it's all the same. Exodus 23:1 (MSG) says, "*Don't pass on malicious gossip. Don't link up with a wicked person and give corrupt testimony.*"

Grab some finger paints and a large paper or roll of paper and gather everyone together. (It's going to get a little messy so plan accordingly. You may want everyone standing on a plastic tablecloth as paint may drip on the floor.) Have everyone stand in a line with their palms together and facing up like they're receiving a gift (either have their hands over a table covered with paper or something covering the floor). Tell them you're going to share something with them. Ask them to stretch out their hands. Fill your hands with washable paint and then grab the hands of the person next to you so they get a generous amount of paint on their palms. Have them then grab the hands of the person next to them in the same way until everyone has paint on their hands. Explain that gossip is like this paint. It stains everyone it touches and colors the way we view people.

If we were to continue on with our day without washing our hands, everything we touch would be affected by the paint. (Have everyone put their hands on the paper to demonstrate.) In order to break free from gossip, we must repent of it—asking God's forgiveness and turning away from it. On the paper where you all put your hands, write, "Spread God's love, not gossip" and display it in your home as a reminder of your family's commitment. Working together, create a list of ideas for spreading God's love in your family, church, and community.

Conversation Connection

» What is gossip? (*Talking about other people*)

» Can you think of a time when gossip hurt you or someone else? What happened?

» Why is gossip wrong?

» What can you do if someone tries to share gossip with you?

Family Fun

Play a game of old-fashioned Telephone. Stand in a line and have the first person quietly whisper something into the ear of the person next to them. That person whispers what they think they heard into the next person's ear. This continues until the message reaches the last person, who shares what they heard aloud. The messages will most likely end up different than what the first person shared. Play as many rounds as you want. Talk about how gossip spreads and hurts each person it touches, and how everyone hears gossip through their own filter, causing it to be distorted as it passes from person to person—so we never want to trust gossip we may hear.

Baking Buddies

Our words can either be sweet or sour. Gossip leaves a sour taste in our hearts and minds. Proverbs 18:21 (AMP) warns us, *"Death and life are in the power of the tongue, and those who love it and indulge it will eat its fruit and bear the consequences of their words."* Today, we're going to make a No Gossip Sour Cake to remind us we will eat the fruit of our words, so we want to choose them wisely.

NO GOSSIP SOUR CAKE

Ingredients

1 box white cake mix
(water, oil, and eggs per box instructions)
2 pkgs (0.13 or 0.14 oz each) strawberry flavored powdered drink mix
½ cup frozen limeade concentrate, thawed

Frosting

1 pkg. (0.13 or 0.14 oz) lemon lime flavored unsweetened drink mix
4-5 tbsp. frozen limeade concentrate, thawed
3 cups powdered sugar
¼ cup butter, softened
1 pkg. sour gummy worms or candies

Directions

Preheat oven to 350ºF (325ºF for dark or nonstick pans).

Spray the bottom of a 13x9" cake pan with cooking spray or grease with butter.

In a large bowl, combine cake mix, water, oil, eggs, and 2 packages of the drink mix. Beat on low speed for 30 seconds, then medium speed for an additional two minutes. Scrape sides of bowl as needed.

Pour batter into prepared pan. Bake 28-35 minutes, or until a toothpick inserted into the center comes out clean.

Allow cake to cool for 15 minutes.

Use a fork or skewer to poke holes all over the top of the cake, approximately ½" apart.

Drizzle ½ cup of the limeade concentrate over the top of the cake. Then allow it to cool completely, approximately 90 minutes.

In a medium bowl, combine 1 pkg. drink mix and 2 tablespoons limeade concentrate until dissolved.

Beat in powdered sugar and butter. Then add an additional teaspoon of the concentrate until the frosting is smooth and spreadable.

Frost the cake, then decorate with the sour candies. Slice and serve.

18

CUSSING/FOUL LANGUAGE

Don't use foul or abusive language.
Let everything you say be good and helpful, so that your words will be
an encouragement to those who hear them.
—Ephesians 4:29

My husband works in logistics for the trucking industry. When James worked in the office, he constantly heard foul language. Eventually, that language came out of his mouth as well. He attempted to curb it at home by *filtering* the cussing, but it still came out as things like, "Son of a biscuit!" or "What the heck?!"

Nothing highlights our negative behavior so much as when we hear it modeled back to us by our young children. So James filtered the foul language further by bleeping it out. Now, instead of the cuss words, our home was filled with, "What the bleep?" and "Bleep, bleep, bleep!" No big deal, right? Wrong. Before we knew it, our nine-year-old daughter was walking around saying, "What the bleep? Bleep, bleep, bleep!" A lot. To other people even!

I explained to her that those bleeps represented cuss words and still weren't appropriate. She responded by saying that *bleeps* were better than saying the words in her head. So, we had to talk about how harmful those types of thoughts are. Even if she didn't say them aloud, they were polluting her heart and mind all the same.

Cussing and foul language are learned behaviors. Whether it's from us as parents, the friends or people our kids hang around with, or the entertainment they watch, our children are learning this toxic talk. Once we form a bad habit, it can take time and consistency to break it.

Some people incorporate things like a swear jar (put money in each time you cuss or use bad language) or an extra chore jar (pull out a piece of paper with a task to complete each time you use bad language) to help break the bad habit. Those types of behavior modification techniques can be helpful but be sure to also spend time drawing nearer to Jesus. The more time we spend reading the Word, praying, and praising, the more our hearts are filled with hope and our minds renewed.

Parents' Prayer

Father God, forgive me for any foul or abusive language that has come out of my own mouth or penetrated my thoughts. Give me wisdom and reveal any things or relationships that are contributing to my child's foul language and help us break free from it. In Jesus's name I pray. Amen.

Teachable Moment

Ephesians 4:29 says, "*Don't use foul or abusive language. Let everything you say be good and helpful, so that your words will be an encouragement to those who hear them.*" We know the Ten Commandments include not misusing the name of God (see Exodus 20:7), but it can be a difficult habit to break, requiring hard work, accountability, and consistency.

Begin by taking responsibility for any foul or abusive language you have used and ask for your child's forgiveness for negatively influencing them. Explain that Proverbs 15:4 (msg) teaches us, "*Kind words heal and help; cutting words wound and maim.*" We want to be people whose words heal and help. First, we must identify the influences in our life contributing to the foul language coming out of our mouths. Let's make a list of some of the sources of that language, such as home, certain TV shows, music, friends, our friends' families, and neighbors. Be specific. It's important to identify where the words have come from.

Next, talk about ways to help change the habit (consider implementing a swear jar or chore jar). Work together to determine the expectations, making sure they are realistic and measurable, and asking for input from your child to create ownership and buy-in.

Finally, discuss coping methods to improve frustration tolerance, emphasizing that what we put into ourselves eventually comes out. Ephesians 5:4 says, "*Obscene stories, foolish talk, and coarse jokes—these are not for you. Instead, let there be thankfulness to God.*" In any situation where we feel frustrated enough to spew foul language, we can instead fill our mouths with thanksgiving.

Conversation Connection

> » Why do you think the Bible warns us not to use foul language or crude joking?

> » Who or what have you been listening to that fuels this type of language?

> » What can you do to change the words you've been using?

> » How can I help to support you?

Family Fun

We are going to play the Choose Your Words Wisely Game. Start with a list of things, animals, people, etc. and write each one on a small piece of paper. One player grabs a slip of paper and then tries to get everyone to guess what's on it by describing it. The only catch is they have to choose their words wisely because they can't say any part of the written word itself. You can choose whether to keep score or play for fun. Give each player a turn.

In the game, we need to think before we speak. We need to choose our words wisely in life as well. Jesus tells us, *"It is not what people put in their mouth that makes them wrong. It is what comes out of their mouth that makes them wrong"* (Matthew 15:11 ERV).

Baking Buddies

> *Words satisfy the mind as much as fruit does the stomach; good talk is as gratifying as a good harvest. Words kill, words give life; they're either poison or fruit—you choose.* (Proverbs 18:20–21 MSG)

Today we're making Cut-It-Out Cookies to remind us to cut out foul language because we will eat the fruit of our words.

CUT-IT-OUT COOKIES

Ingredients

2 sticks (1 cup) unsalted butter, softened
⅔ cup powdered sugar (plus 3 tbsp., separated)
1 large egg yolk
1 tsp. vanilla extract
2 ½ cups all-purpose flour
¼ tsp. salt
⅔ cup raspberry jam
Also need plastic wrap and two cookie cutters (different sizes of same shape: heart, star, circle, etc.)

Directions

Preheat oven to 325ºF. Line two baking sheets with parchment paper.

In the bowl of your stand mixer (or other large mixing bowl), beat butter and 2/3 cup of powdered sugar until fluffy.

Add in egg yolk and vanilla and beat until combined.

Mix in flour and salt until dough is incorporated.

Separate dough into two balls and place each on a piece of plastic wrap. Flatten balls into disks and cover each one in the plastic wrap.

Refrigerate dough for at least one hour.

Spread a handful of flour on a clean counter and place one disk on floured surface. Use a rolling pin to roll dough out to approximately 1/8" thick. Cut out shapes with the larger cookie cutter.

Use the smaller cookie cutter to cut out a window in half of the cookies.

Use a spatula to carefully transfer the cookies to your prepared baking sheets.

Grab the scraps of dough, form it into a ball, and place it back in the plastic wrap. Refrigerate it while you roll out the other disk of dough as it is sticky and you want the cookies to maintain their shape. *If cookies get too warm, you can place the cookie sheet in the fridge or freezer for 10 minutes to chill before placing them in the oven so they hold their shape better.*

Bake cookies for 8-12 minutes, just until the edges are golden brown. Allow them to cool for 5 minutes before transferring to a wire cooling rack.

Repeat process with the second disk. If you don't have enough cookie sheets, wait to roll out the second disk until the first batch is out of the oven. You want your dough to remain chilled so the cookies maintain their shape.

Spread ¾ tsp. jam over the flat side of the cookies without the cut-out windows. Top them with the remaining cookies (flat side down) so the jam shows through the cut-outs.

Gently sift the remaining 3 tbsp. of powdered sugar over the cookies and enjoy.

19

STEALING

~♡♡♡~

You shall not steal
[secretly, openly, fraudulently, or through carelessness].
—Exodus 20:15 (AMP)

I still recall walking out of a corner store as a college student with a forgotten tube of lip gloss in my hand alongside my keys. I walked right past the cashier and through the security detectors. It wasn't until I got to my car that I realized what I had done. I panicked and rushed back into the store to pay for the makeup.

Before you start thinking how honest and amazing I am, you should also know that I didn't think twice about bringing home some office supplies as a young professional cleaning out my desk. You see, I hadn't been saved yet. I didn't consider that taking those pens or sticky notes was stealing. However, somewhere along my journey, I realized that what I had done was wrong and repented for it. I had violated one of the Ten Commandments.

How about you? Have you ever taken something that didn't belong to you, intentionally or unintentionally? What about leaving the grocery store and later realizing either you or the cashier failed to ring up one of your items? Or how about doing something personal while on the clock, which is essentially stealing your employer's time? What about failing to report income on your taxes when you sell something at a garage sale or receive some other type of reportable income?

During college, I spent several years working as a juvenile probation officer. I encountered many kids and teens who stole—some for pleasure, some for the thrill, and some because they felt entitled. Others stole out of a feeling of desperate need. Still others simply wanted attention. Each time, it was important for me to get to the root cause of their behavior; otherwise, they would continue to steal.

If your child is stealing, be sure to explore the heart behind the behavior and not just the behavior itself. Otherwise, like a weed whose roots remain in the soil, it will continue to grow and may even lead to something worse. Understanding the root cause of any behavioral issue will help you pave a path forward to freedom.

Parents' Prayer

Jesus, reveal the root cause of my child's stealing. Give me the words to speak to get to the heart of the matter and wisdom to help my child break free from this sin. Amen.

Teachable Moment

Choose your child's most prized possession. Grab it and call your child to the table. Explain to them that you've decided you really want it, so you're taking it and keeping it (*Warning: they'll likely throw a massive fit.*) Ask how they feel about you taking something of theirs without permission. Then ask how they think the owner of whatever they've stolen likely feels.

Explain that the Bible is very clear that stealing is a sin. It breaks one of the Ten Commandments. Exodus 20:15 states: *"You must not steal."* Another version (AMP) specifies, *"You shall not steal [secretly, openly, fraudulently, or through carelessness]."* The Bible also tells us, *"Wealth gained by doing wrong will not really help you, but doing right will save you from death"* (Proverbs 10:2 ERV).

While stealing may not seem like that big of a deal, God says it *is* a big deal. The Bible even specifically addresses stealing from your parents:

Anyone who steals from his father and mother and says, "What's wrong with that?" is no better than a murderer. (Proverbs 28:24)

Study the story of Achan in Joshua 7. (It's a bit graphic for young kids as Achan and his family are killed after he stole some treasure set apart for the Lord. You can summarize the story by explaining that his stealing cost him and his family their lives or just say he was brought before Joshua and the community for punishment. You can also emphasize that God had not yet sent Jesus to die for our sins, and that now that He has, we don't see the same types of punishments because Jesus paid the price for our sins on the cross. However, we still have to repent and live with the consequences of our choices.)

Explore how Achan's behavior impacted not just himself and his family, but his entire community. Discuss ways your child's thefts have negatively affected them, your family, and others. Depending on your child's age, you could also talk about laws and how their behavior could lead to restrictions on their freedom, juvenile jail, or having a lifelong record that could hurt their future chances for a job, college, or even renting an apartment.

Conversation Connection

» Have you ever suffered from something someone else did? How did it make you feel?

» How do you think your behavior has hurt others? What can you do to try to make things right?

» Why do you think God emphasized the importance of not stealing by making it one of the Ten Commandments?

» What can you do to keep from stealing the next time you're tempted?

Family Fun

Play an old-fashioned game of Cops and Robbers together. Decide who will be cops and who will be robbers. The robbers hide or run around trying to evade the cops. When they are caught, they're "jailed" for a minute, after which they become cops. Meanwhile, the cop who nabbed that person becomes a robber. When you're done playing, remind your kids what Isaiah 61:8 says: *"For I, the LORD, love justice. I hate robbery and wrongdoing. I will faithfully reward my people for their suffering and make an everlasting covenant with them."*

Baking Buddies

The Bible instructs us in Ephesians 4:28: *"If you are a thief, quit stealing. Instead, use your hands for good hard work, and then give generously to others in need."* So, today we are making No More Sticky Fingers Toffee Pudding to remind us to use our hands for good hard work instead of stealing.

NO MORE STICKY FINGERS TOFFEE PUDDING

Ingredients

4-6 oz. dried, pitted dates, roughly chopped
1 cup boiling water
1 tsp. baking soda
½ cup dark brown sugar
¼ cup unsalted butter, softened to room temperature
1 tbsp. oil
1 tbsp. dark molasses or black treacle
1 tsp. pure vanilla extract
1 ½ cups all-purpose flour
1 ¼ tsp. baking powder
½ tsp. salt
**Additional 8 tbsp. brown sugar and 3 tbsp. butter to line the bottom of each cupcake tin.

Toffee Sauce

1 cup heavy cream
1 cup dark brown sugar
½ cup unsalted butter
Pinch of salt
1 tsp. pure vanilla extract

Directions

Chop the dates into smaller pieces and place in a small bowl.

Pour boiling water over the dates and stir in the baking soda. Allow the dates to soak and cool down.

Place the dates in a blender or food processor (or use an immersion blender if you have one) in order to puree the dates—but don't fully puree them as you want the mixture to still be somewhat chunky, not smooth.

Preheat oven to 350°F.

In a large mixing bowl, cream together the butter and brown sugar until smooth.

Beat in the eggs and oil, then add the molasses (or black treacle) and vanilla extract until combined.

In a small bowl, whisk together the flour, baking powder, and salt.

Gradually beat the dry ingredients into the wet ingredients, just until combined.

Add the chunky date mixture and stir it together.

Use the giant-sized muffin tins (they hold approximately one cup of batter). Butter the pan or use a non-stick spray to coat each one so they don't stick. (*Or you could use 12 regular-sized muffin tins or an 8x8" cake pan if needed.*)

Place 2 tsp. of brown sugar at the bottom of each tin and ¼ tbsp. of butter (if baking in a cake pan, spread the brown sugar evenly over the cake pan and dot with small chunks of the butter before pouring the batter over top).

Using a giant cookie or ice cream scoop, fill each muffin tin approximately 2/3 full.

Bake on the center rack for approximately 25 minutes (*reduce time to 10-18 minutes if you use smaller muffin pans or increase time to 35-40 minutes if using an 8x8" cake pan instead*). You want a toothpick inserted into the center to come out clean.

Allow the cakes to cool for several minutes in the tins, then remove them and place on a wire rack to finish cooling. Gently run a butter knife around the edges to remove if they're sticking.

To make the sticky sauce, place the heavy cream, brown sugar, salt, and butter in a medium-sized sauce pan over medium heat. *Resist the temptation to stir at this point. You want to allow the sugar to dissolve completely to avoid splashing up the sides, which causes the sauce to turn grainy.*

As soon as the brown sugar dissolves, increase the heat to medium-high, stirring only occasionally to avoid it burning. As the sauce browns, increase the frequency of your stirring to prevent it from burning. The sauce is done when it turns a dark brown and thickens. You can decide when to take it off depending on the consistency and depth of flavor you prefer.

Once you remove it from the heat, stir in the vanilla extract. If it gets too thick, you can add a little more butter or heavy cream and reheat it to thin it out.

Place the pudding cake on a plate and drizzle with the toffee sauce before serving. You can also add a bit of ice cream or a drizzle of cream on top if desired.

20

LYING

*Does anyone want to live a life that is long and prosperous? Then keep
your tongue from speaking evil and your lips from telling lies!*
—Psalm 34:12–13

I didn't do it."

"I don't know how that happened."

"It wasn't me!"

Why is it that lying comes so naturally to us—and to our kids? Over
the years, this is an issue we've addressed numerous times with both of our
kids. Sometimes, fear or shame cause people to lie, tell a half-truth, or even
simply omit the truth. But no matter what the reason, lying is lying, and
it's wrong.

In order to encourage our kids to be honest—regardless of how bad a
situation may seem—we've always emphasized that the consequences for
lying will be more severe than if they immediately tell us the truth. By committing to controlling our own emotions and reactions as parents, it has
also helped our kids learn it's always safe to be truthful. It hasn't been easy,

mind you, but it's definitely helped us overcome the propensity for lying... most of the time anyway.

Another aspect of this issue is overexaggerating or stretching the truth. Our daughter especially has a flair for the dramatic and is an excellent storyteller. However, we've had to work with her to help her understand the importance of sharing truthfully in order to build and maintain trust with others.

After a period in which Kendra lied frequently to avoid getting into trouble, our trust with her was severely damaged. I constantly questioned whether she was telling the truth. She'd get frustrated and ask why I didn't believe her, so I had to explain that being honest is the only way to regain our trust.

Parents' Prayer

Heavenly Father, forgive me for times I have lied. Increase my self-control when catching my children in a lie and equip me to help them walk in truth. In Jesus's name I pray. Amen.

Teachable Moment

The first lies told on earth came from the mouth of the serpent in the garden of Eden. He asked Eve, *"Did God really say you must not eat the fruit from any of the trees in the garden?"* (Genesis 3:1), knowing full well that this wasn't the case. When Eve explained that God said she and Adam were allowed to eat everything except for the fruit from one certain tree, of which God said, *"You must not eat it or even touch it; if you do, you will die"* (verse 3), the serpent replied:

> *"You won't die!...God knows that your eyes will be opened as soon as you eat it, and you will be like God, knowing both good and evil."*
>
> (Genesis 3:4–5)

This is why Satan is known as *"the father of lies"* (John 8:44). When we lie, we partner with Satan. God feels strongly about lying, but He is merciful to forgive us when we ask for it. There are many stories in the Bible of mighty men and women of God who lied at one time or another.

For younger kids, read the story of Zacchaeus in Luke 19:1–10 and explain that Zacchaeus was a tax collector who got rich by being dishonest. After encountering Jesus, however, he had a radical change of heart and chose to give half of his money away to the poor and pay people back four times the amount he took from them.

For older kids, read the story of Ananias and Sapphira in Acts 5:1–11 and discuss why this couple's actions meant they were lying to God. Explain that while God hates lying, He loves us. In fact, He sent His Son Jesus to defeat the power of sin forever because of His great love for us.

Here are some additional biblical stories about lying to study if you choose. Your kids can explore what motivated the person to lie and the consequences: Abraham lied to Pharaoh (Genesis 12:11–20); Sarah lied to God (Genesis 18:15); Abraham lied to Abimelech (Genesis 20:1–16); Isaac lied to the men of Gerar (Genesis 26:6–11); Jacob lied to Isaac (Genesis 27:19–45); Laban lied to Jacob (Genesis 29:14–28); Jacob's sons lied to him about Joseph (Genesis 37:18–36); and Potiphar's wife lied to Potiphar about Joseph (Genesis 39:1–23). Note how God blessed Joseph even when he was in prison.

Conversation Connection

- » Why is lying harmful?

- » Is it a lie if you don't say anything when you know you should?

- » How does lying hurt friendships and other relationships?

- » How can you tell the truth even when you're afraid of getting in trouble?

Family Fun

Play the game Two Truths and a Lie. Ask each person to think of three things to share about themselves, two that are true and one that isn't true. Everyone else guesses which one is false. Explain: "In this game, we know one of the statements is false, but how would it feel to be told a lie if it wasn't a game? In our family, let's commit to always tell the truth." The Bible teaches us just how strongly God feels about lying:

> The LORD hates these seven things: eyes that show pride, tongues that tell lies, hands that kill innocent people, hearts that plan evil things to do, feet that run to do evil, witnesses in court who tell lies, and anyone who causes family members to fight. (Proverbs 6:16–19 ERV)

> The LORD detests lying lips, but he delights in those who tell the truth. (Proverbs 12:22)

Baking Buddies

Because God delights in the truth, we're making Delightful Truthful Truffles today to remind us how sweet the truth is.

DELIGHTFUL TRUTHFUL TRUFFLES

Ingredients

2 quality semisweet or dark chocolate bars (4 oz. each)
⅔ cup heavy cream (full fat coconut milk can be substituted if needed)
1 tbsp. unsalted butter, softened
½ tsp. pure vanilla extract
Toppings of choice: sprinkles, crushed nuts, unsweetened cocoa powder, melted white chocolate or other chocolate, toffee bits, etc.

Directions

Finely chop the chocolate and place in a medium-sized microwave safe bowl. Set aside.

In a medium saucepan over medium-high, heat the heavy cream until simmering (or you can microwave it in a microwave-safe bowl in 30 second increments until simmering).

Place butter over top of chocolate, then pour the heavy cream evenly over the top of the chocolate and butter.

Allow the mixture to sit for five minutes.

Add the vanilla extract and then stir until the chocolate melts completely.

Pour mixture into an 8x8" baking dish or pie pan so it can set quickly and evenly.

Place plastic wrap directly on the top surface of the chocolate mix and refrigerate for 1-2 hours.

Use a cookie scoop to scoop the mixture into a mound and roll it into a ball, then roll it into the topping of choice. *The mixture will be sticky, so you can use plastic gloves or dust your hands lightly with cocoa powder before rolling. Or, you can scoop the mounds onto a baking sheet lined with parchment paper and refrigerate for an additional 20-30 minutes before rolling into balls and coating with toppings if you prefer.

I also utilize the stickiness to remind my kids that lies tend to get us into sticky situations, which is another reason why we always want to tell the truth.

Store the truffles in the fridge if not eaten immediately.

21

WHINING/COMPLAINING

Do everything without complaining and arguing.
—Philippians 2:14

Ugh. My eye twitches just thinking about all the times my kids whine and complain. At the age of six, my son seemed to hit a stage where he whined more than he spoke. When we asked him to do something, he would whine, complain, and then whine some more.

It felt like an endless loop without reprieve. Some of his complaints were things he'd heard from his older sister, but I have no idea where the rest came from. It was out of control!

As we went through the process of redirecting the behavior, I realized Jordan wasn't the only one guilty of this. I may not have sounded as peevish as my son (at least not to my own ears), but the Holy Spirit convicted me of my complaining all the same. I realized after a long road trip and living out of hotels for several weeks that I was no longer focused on gratitude but grumbling. In fact, I even found fault with our brand-new home. Can you believe it?!

God had done many miraculous things to get us across the country and into our beautiful new house, but I couldn't help but compare it to our previous home. I saw all of the little construction flaws instead of focusing my heart on thanksgiving for all the blessings in front of me. And I realized just how easy it truly is to veer off-course into a gully of grumbling.

Perhaps it's the food or service at a restaurant, the way someone treats us or our kids, or traffic, bosses, spouses, relatives, coworkers…or a million other little things. I know I'm guilty of complaining about these things. Maybe you struggle some with this too? Perhaps, unlike me, you don't share them aloud. Did you know that even if we don't voice those complaints, thinking them has the same effect—it causes a bitter root to spring forth.

Whining and complaining may not seem like the biggest issue in the world, but it caused the Israelites to wander in the desert for forty years instead of entering their promised land—which tells me it's a very big deal to God. We've got to tackle the moaning and groaning as soon as it rears its ugly head. It's a lot like dandelions actually; if we allow it to take root, we'll have a yard full of weeds that quickly spread to those around us as well.

Parents' Prayer

Father God, forgive me for complaining and whining. Help me to live a life of thanksgiving and teach my kids to do the same. In Jesus's name I pray. Amen.

Teachable Moment

The Bible tells us, "*Do everything without complaining and arguing, so that no one can criticize you. Live clean, innocent lives as children of God, shining like bright lights in a world full of crooked and perverse people*" (Philippians 2:14–15).

We're going to work on turning our grumbling into gratitude. When we whine, complain, or grumble, it grieves God. Did you know grumbling got the Israelites into a lot of trouble in the wilderness? You've heard the story of how God brought the Israelites out of Egypt with many miracles—sending plagues to the Egyptians, parting the Red Sea, and feeding the Israelites with manna from heaven—but did you know that their journey was supposed to be very short? Because they were obstinate, disobedient, and forgot God's promises, a trip that could have taken just eleven days lasted for forty years—and an entire generation of people didn't even get to enter the promised land after all that wandering. Whining and complaining distract us from our destiny.

So, today we're going to work on strategies for overcoming complaining. Philippians 4:6–7 teaches us what we should do instead of whining and complaining:

> *Don't worry about anything; instead, pray about everything. Tell God what you need, and thank him for all he has done. Then you will experience God's peace, which exceeds anything we can understand. His peace will guard your hearts and minds as you live in Christ Jesus.*

When we feel upset, we can pray and tell God what we need, then thank Him for all He has done for us. When we focus on being grateful for His blessings, we no longer feel the urge to whine and complain because we can focus on the truth that we can trust God with the big and small details of our lives.

Let's practice. Think of the last time you whined or complained. Now let's pray and tell God what we need. Notice, the Bible doesn't say we should whine about how unfair the situation was or complain about someone else. It says we are supposed to *tell God what we need.* This takes some practice because we've got to stop and think about the situation. Do we need to feel heard? Do we need to feel safe? Do we need to set a boundary?

If you aren't sure exactly what you need, pray and ask God to help you figure it out. The Bible teaches us in James 1:5 that we can ask God for wisdom anytime, and He will give it to us. It's always safe to talk to God and ask for help.

Next, we need to start thanking God for all He's done. Let's practice this. We'll take turns and see how many reasons we have to be thankful. Let's start a gratitude list. (Kids can write or draw pictures depending on their ages.) This will help us so the next time we feel like whining or complaining, we have a list ready to help us grow in gratitude. We can add to the list each time we find ourselves grumbling.

For older kids, take time to go through Exodus, particularly chapters 3–17 and 32, as well as Numbers 11–21. Explore all of the ways the Israelites complained and how it negatively impacted their journey through the wilderness. Be sure to note that while some of God's responses may seem harsh, God always heard Moses's pleas, and He sent His Son Jesus to bear our sins and provide hope in Him.

Conversation Connection

- » Why do you think it's wrong to whine and complain?

- » How do you think God feels when we complain instead of being grateful?

- » What can we do when we feel upset and want to whine or complain?

- » How can I help you when you start to whine or complain? What do you need from me in those situations?

Family Fun

Let's play the Grateful Game. Take turns sharing something for which you are thankful or grateful. There's just one rule: you can't repeat what someone else has already said. (You can choose whether someone is "out" of the game if they can't think of anything new.) For a more challenging variation, share gratitude in A-to-Z style. Each person must share something starting with the next letter. If they can't, they're out. Keep going through the alphabet until only one person remains. Set a 3-5 second time limit if needed. (This can be fun. We can be grateful for everything from apples to zebras!)

Baking Buddies

The Bible warns us, *"Do everything without grumbling or arguing"* (Philippians 2:14 NIV). Grumbling grieves our good and generous God. We want to grow in gratitude instead of griping, so today we're making a Grumble-Free Galette to remind us to guard our hearts against complaining.

GRUMBLE-FREE GALETTE

Ingredients

For an even easier recipe, you can also buy the ready-made pie dough instead of making it from scratch. It's quick and delicious.

Pie Crust

1 ½ cups all-purpose flour
2 tsp. granulated sugar
½ tsp. salt
1 ½ sticks (12 tbsp.) unsalted butter (cut into thin slices)
4-5 tbsp. cold water

Filling

4 cups fruit of choice (*we love pitted cherries or mixed fruit—strawberries, blueberries, and raspberries—but you can use fruit of choice; just be sure to thinly slice fruits like apples and pears so they cook thoroughly*)
⅓ cup granulated sugar (you can use up to ½ cup if you prefer it sweeter or are using especially tart fruit)
2 tbsp. cornstarch
2 tsp. lemon juice

Egg Wash

1 large egg
2 tsp. cold water

Directions

If making with store-bought crust, skip down to filling instructions.

In a food processor, pulse flour, sugar, and salt until combined. If you don't have a good processor, you can also whisk them together in a large bowl.

Add in the thinly sliced butter chunks and pulse until it comes together in a coarse mixture (or you can use a pastry cutter or cut apart with two forks to incorporate the butter).

Sprinkle mixture with 4 tbsp. of cold water and pulse until it comes together as a dough, adding in the fifth or last tbsp. only if needed to make the dough form.

Remove the dough from the food processor and shape into a flat, round disk. Wrap it in plastic wrap and refrigerate for 30 minutes to chill the dough.

Filling:

In a large bowl, combine your fruits (be sure to thoroughly dry fruit with a paper towel after rinsing to remove excess moisture), sugar, cornstarch, and lemon juice, stirring to combine.

Preheat oven to 400°F.

Place chilled dough on a large piece of parchment paper and use a rolling pin to roll it out into a 12" circle. If using a store-bought crust, simply remove from package and unroll onto the parchment paper.

Scoop fruit mixture into the center of the dough, leaving a 2-3" border around the edges without any fruit.

Fold the sides of the dough up over the edges of the fruit, folding it over itself as needed to make a sealed edge all around. The fruit in the middle will be exposed and it will look like a rustic bowl.

Explain to your kids: "Just as we're folding the edges up to protect the fruit in our galette, we want to wrap our hearts and minds in gratitude to guard against grumbling. I'm grateful for this time together. What are you grateful for right now?"

In a small bowl, whisk together the egg and 2 tbsp. cold water. Brush the egg wash evenly over the folded crust and discard the rest of the egg wash. *This helps give the crust a golden shine.*

Grab the parchment paper with the galette and place on a cookie sheet. Bake for 35-45 minutes, until the fruit filling is bubbly and the crust is golden brown. Serve warm and feel free to add a scoop of ice cream or a dollop of whipped cream if desired.

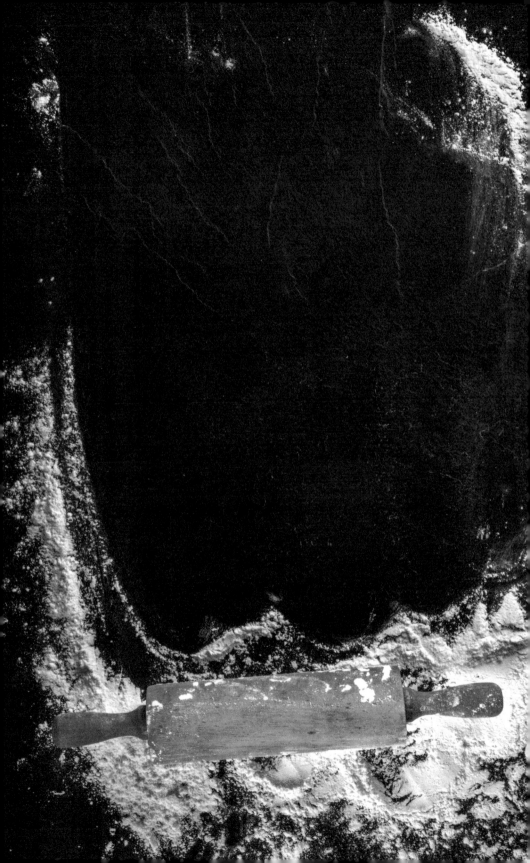

22

CHEATING

We reject all shameful deeds and underhanded methods. We don't try to trick anyone or distort the word of God. We tell the truth before God, and all who are honest know this.
—2 Corinthians 4:2

Our daughter was born with a competitive spirit. She hated losing at games; even from a young age, she tried to cheat to win. Now, being super competitive myself, as well as the reigning game champion of my family, that didn't sit well with me.

I'd love to say my motives were altruistic and I was being a great mom by trying to teach my child right from wrong, but I'd be lying. To me, the only thing worse than losing a game was losing to a cheater—that set off my justice meter like crazy! So, I quickly squashed the idea that cheating was okay.

Now, I'm not a completely terrible mom. There were times I worked hard to let her win too.

I wish I could say I've never cheated at a game or an assignment or cut a corner to get ahead, but again, I'd be lying. The temptation to cheat is all around us. The right thing is rarely the easy one. As we face pressures in life, fear sets in, and the temptation can feel too great to bear. But the Bible teaches us:

> *The temptations in your life are no different from what others experi-*
> *ence. And God is faithful. He will not allow the temptation to be more*
> *than you can stand. When you are tempted, he will show you a way out*
> *so that you can endure.* (1 Corinthians 10:13)

Combating the propensity to cheat requires self-control and a desire to do the right thing. I've found in discipling my kids that it's not enough to just give them a list of rules and behaviors they should follow in order to be righteous. Instead, I help them identify and seek to live a life of purpose. When we focus on the *desired* behaviors instead of merely fighting the undesirable ones, we instill biblical character traits in our kids to help guide their lives. An endless list of *what not to do* is not enough. You'll build a stronger relationship with your children and a firmer foundation of faith by teaching them who they were created to become instead of focusing primarily on their shortcomings.

Parents' Prayer

God, forgive me for times I have acted dishonestly. Help me to walk in integrity and teach my kids to do the same. In Jesus's name I pray. Amen.

Teachable Moment

Play your kids' favorite board game together, but when it's your turn, cheat in a very obvious way. (For instance, if you are playing Monopoly and you're the banker, keep taking extra "cash.") When your child complains, acknowledge that you were cheating and ask why it upsets them. Explain that anytime we act dishonestly or unfairly to try to get what we want, we are cheating. The Bible tells us, "God *hates cheating in the marketplace;* *he loves it when business is aboveboard*" (Proverbs 11:1 MSG). If your child is very young, you may need to point out your cheating. (For example, "I rolled a 2 but I'm going to cheat and go 10 so I can win instead of you. How do you feel about that? Is it fair to cheat? Is it kind to cheat?")

There are lots of ways people cheat in life. Let's make a list of some ways (cheating at games, taking or keeping more money than you should, looking at someone else's answers and copying their work, etc.). The Bible warns us, *"Money gained by cheating others will soon be gone. Money earned through hard work will grow and grow"* (Proverbs 13:11 ERV).

For a biblical story of someone who cheated, read about Jacob cheating his twin brother Esau out of his blessing in Genesis 27:1–41. You can talk about how even though Jacob lied and cheated, God still loved him and had good plans for him. This will help your child understand that even though they've struggled with this behavior, they don't have to be defined by it, and they can make different choices moving forward. To equip them to break free from any shame or unworthiness, read and discuss Romans 5:8–11:

But God showed us his great love for us by sending Christ to die for us while we were still sinners. And since we have been made right in God's sight by the blood of Christ, he will certainly save us from God's condemnation. For since our friendship with God was restored by the death of his Son while we were still his enemies, we will certainly be saved through the life of his Son. So now we can rejoice in our wonderful new relationship with God because our Lord Jesus Christ has made us friends of God.

Instead of cheating, God wants us to deal honestly with people in every situation, to do what's right even when no one is looking.

Conversation Connection

» What are some of the situations where we might be tempted to cheat?

» Why do people cheat?

» How can we fight the urge to cheat?

» What can you do to help you deal honestly with people?

Family Fun

Choose a favorite family board game to play and add another dimension to it by playing Cheating Chimpanzee. Rip a piece of paper into smaller pieces, one for each person playing. Write "cheating chimpanzee" on one piece and leave the others blank or put a smiley face or another word on these. (This all depends on how discerning your family is; mine would see one paper had writing and the others didn't.) Fold the papers and have each person draw one to find out who will be the *cheating chimpanzee* during that round of the game.

Play the board game as usual, but the *cheating chimpanzee* will try to cheat without getting caught. The other players try to discover who the cheater is. When they catch the person, they call out, "Cheating chimpanzee!" Then draw new papers and continue playing. Warn everyone not to falsely accuse someone of being the *cheating chimpanzee*. You can keep score of who catches the cheater or not; it's up to you.

At the end, talk about how much more fun it is to play with honest people and not have to worry about whether someone is cheating. God doesn't like when we cheat either. The Bible says:

> Yes, always use honest weights and measures, so that you may enjoy a long life in the land the LORD your God is giving you. All who cheat with dishonest weights and measures are detestable to the LORD your God. (Deuteronomy 25:15–16)

Baking Buddies

The Bible teaches us, "It is sin to know what you **ought** to do and then not do it" (James 4:17). We know that cheating in any way is a sin, which is why we're making Cheaters Never Prosper Carrot Cake today. We want to choose to do the right thing even when it's challenging.

CHEATERS NEVER PROSPER CARROT CAKE

Ingredients

2 cups all-purpose flour
2 tsp. baking soda
½ tsp. sea salt
1 ½ tsp. ground cinnamon
1 ¼ cups canola or vegetable oil
1 cup granulated sugar
1 cup lightly packed brown sugar
1 tsp. vanilla extract
4 large eggs (room temperature is best)
3 cups peeled & grated carrots (approximately 5-6 medium-sized carrots)
1 cup chopped pecans (optional)
½ cup raisins (optional)

Frosting

8 oz. cream cheese (softened to room temperature)
1 ¼ cup powdered sugar
⅓ cup heavy whipping cream
½ cup chopped pecans to top the cake with (optional)

Directions

This recipe can make a two-layer 9" round cake or approximately 24 cupcakes. You could also use a 9x13" cake pan if preferred (but baking time would increase).

Begin by spraying two 9" round pans with cooking spray. Cut circles of parchment paper to line the bottoms with (**TIP:** use a pencil and draw a circle around the bottom of the pan and then cut them out slightly smaller than your pencil marks so they fit inside the pans). Then spray more cooking spray over the top of the parchment in the pans. *Or, if you're doing cupcakes, line the cupcake pans with paper liners.*

Preheat oven to 350°F.

In a medium bowl, whisk together the flour, baking soda, salt, and cinnamon until blended. Set aside.

In a large bowl or the bowl of your stand mixer, whisk together the oil, sugars, and vanilla.

Beat the eggs in one at a time.

Slowly add the dry ingredients into the wet ones, stirring until fully combined.

Stir in the carrots, nuts and raisins.

Pour half the cake into each of the round pans or fill cupcake liners approximately 2/3 full.

Bake round cakes for 35-40 minutes or until a toothpick inserted into the middle comes out clean. If making cupcakes, bake for 12-18 minutes.

Allow the cakes to cool in the pans for approximately 15 minutes. Place a cooling rack over the top of the cake pan and carefully flip it over to remove cake onto rack. Gently peel off parchment paper. Repeat with the other pan. *If making cupcakes, wait approximately 5-10 minutes before removing from pan to cooling racks.

Allow the cakes to cool completely before frosting.

Frosting:

In a large bowl or the bowl of your stand mixer, beat the cream cheese for approximately one minute (use a hand mixer if you don't have a stand mixer), until creamy.

Beat the powdered sugar in little by little until fluffy.

Pour in the whipping cream and beat on medium speed for 2-3 minutes, until the frosting is creamy and fluffy.

Cover and chill the frosting until you are ready to frost the cake.

Place one cake on a cake stand or flat serving platter with the flat bottom side up. Use a spatula or butter knife to frost just the top and then place the second layer on top with the flat side up. Frost just the top again and garnish with a few of the chopped pecans. Slice and enjoy.

If making cupcakes, you can either use a spatula to spread the frosting, or you can place it in a piping bag with a tip for more decoration. You can also place frosting in a small plastic bag and cut a tiny hole in one of the bottom corners to create quick and easy piping bags for the kids to decorate the cupcakes with.

13

POOR CHOICES

There's a way of life that looks harmless enough; look again—it leads straight to hell. Sure, those people appear to be having a good time, but all that laughter will end in heartbreak.
—Proverbs 14:12–13 (MSG)

We went through a period when our kids consistently made poor choices. Whether it's testing boundaries, being with the wrong people or in bad situations, seeking attention, or simply not knowing better, the choices we make in life can have significant repercussions.

As we equip our children to become wise decision makers, we prepare them to thrive in all areas of their lives. I'd love to tell you it happens naturally over time, but you just have to go on social media or look around to see that many people never learn how to make good choices. This means it's our responsibility to teach our kids how to consider their options and act accordingly.

However, it's not enough to just try to make the right choices. We want to prepare our children to know how to walk with God through the decision-making process. Faith requires action, and the actions required by faith often fall outside of what would logically be considered a wise decision. We simply have to look at the lives of Noah, David, Abraham, Paul, Esther, Rahab, or even Jesus to realize that the choices we make in faith often contradict what we know in the natural.

My husband and I have been putting this type of biblical decision-making process into practice for over fifteen years now. We've done a lot of things that appear crazy to the world or made no earthly sense, and yet we've experienced the miraculous in and through our lives, and the lives of those we influence, because of the choices we've made.

Don't get me wrong. It isn't easy. We've had family, friends, and even pastors attempt to talk us out of some of the best choices we've ever made—not out of spite or malice, but simply out of their deep love and concern for us because, to them, these choices didn't seem safe or make sense.

Like the time we chose to accept a youth pastor's position across the state—for a group that had barely any youth, in a location where we knew no one, and with a salary offer that wasn't enough to provide for our family. We could have accepted a position in our hometown with a full youth group under a pastor we knew and loved. That easy route would have kept us in our comfort zone, near family and friends, but by stepping out in faith, we learned to trust God for everything. As a result, we experienced greater miracles in that season than we ever had before. Countless lives were changed because we were willing to obey God instead of man.

Another time, we sold our home less than two years after purchasing it to build a home in a neighboring city. Less than a year later, God asked us to sell the new house and move across the country. Neither move made sense at the time, but looking back, we see how powerfully God worked in and through those choices. We're still experiencing the fruit of those decisions today.

I'm thankful that even at their young ages, our children have already encountered miracle after miracle and answered prayer upon answered prayer because of our faith walk. It has helped to show them how to wrestle through these types of choices themselves.

You see, we don't just make these kinds of choices off in our prayer closets by ourselves. No. We involve our kids every step of the way. We talk about what we're thinking, feeling, praying, and considering. It's in this type of modeling and engagement that our kids get to learn and experience biblical decision-making so they can begin applying it to their own lives. Because the truth is, we can't effectively teach our kids something we aren't living ourselves.

Parents' Prayer

Jesus, thank You for being Lord of my life. Teach me to walk with You to make the best choices for my life and my family's lives. Equip me to show my kids how to implement biblical decision-making skills as well. Amen.

Teachable Moment

Have you ever made a choice that led to consequences you didn't like? I think we all have. Today we're going to look at some of the choices people in the Bible made in order to learn how to make the best decisions we can for our own lives.

Noah made a decision to build an ark on dry land when he had never experienced a flood before. (See Genesis 6:9–9:17; Hebrews 11:7.) It took Noah a lot of time and hard work to follow through on his choice to trust and obey God in this. It required faith in his decision-making process. What would have happened if he had made a different choice? Aren't you glad he made the wise choice to obey God even when it didn't make a lot of sense?

Can you think of other people in the Bible who made choices that may not have seemed wise to others but were in obedience to God or were faith-filled actions that changed the world? Let's make of list of other people in the Bible whose choices changed our world as we know it—both wise choices and poor choices. (Divide a paper in half lengthwise and write "wise choices" and "poor choices" at the tops of the two columns.)

Then, brainstorm together as many as you can. Once you've filled your list, go through and talk about why each of the poor choices made it on that list. What do they all have in common? (This may include disobedience to God, impulsivity, seeking their own benefit or satisfaction over the good of others, not asking for or following wise counsel, not thinking through the potential consequences first, etc.) How about the wise decisions (the person was close to God, prayed, obeyed God, considered the good of others, operated in faith, tried something new, sought wise counsel, etc.)? You may wish to go through a children's Bible story by story for this activity.

Based on what we've learned, let's write out (or draw for younger kids) a guide to biblical decision-making to help us make better choices. You can create your own or utilize this as a guide:

1. Think about all the possible choices in this situation.

2. Consider potential consequences (good and bad) of each choice, including who could be impacted by the choice and in what ways. Be sure to think of immediate consequences and long-term consequences.

3. Ask yourself what the Bible has to say about the matter (talk to your parents or pastor if you need help figuring this out, search the keyword in the back of your Bible, or search the Internet for applicable Scriptures).

4. Pray about it and ask God for wisdom. (See James 1:5.)

5. Seek wise and godly counsel from a trusted adult

6. Move forward with the best possible choice, but don't be afraid to pause and pivot if it turns out to be the wrong choice.

For more about what biblical decision-making looks like, you can also study Hebrews 11 and discuss the choices each of the great men and women of the Bible made in faith.

Conversation Connection

» How do our choices impact our lives?

» Have you ever made a choice that you regretted? Tell me about it. What did you learn from that experience?

» What do you think it means to use a biblical decision-making process?

» How can I help you when you're facing a difficult choice?

Family Fun

We're going to play the Which Cup Game. Grab three to five foam cups or other non-breakable cups that you can't see through. On pieces of paper, write out different consequences—some fun, some silly, and some that involve work. Ideas may include: do a silly dance; sing your favorite song at the top of your lungs; do your sibling's chores for the day; clean a specific room; eat dessert before dinner; do an act of kindness for someone today; wear your underwear on your head; tell your most embarrassing moment; scrub all the toilets; or eat something you don't like. Fold each paper up and place one under each cup; you can keep any extra options for additional rounds. Have each child take turns choosing which cup to lift up. Explain that they get to choose the cup, but they are expected to do whatever the paper says—no matter what.

If you wish, you can also list unsafe behaviors on some papers and if your child selects one of those, ask them what they're going to do. Choosing to refuse to do what's on the paper even though they agreed to the rules of the game is the right decision. The Bible shows us that we never want to go against what God says. Celebrate the wise choice and let them know they get a reward for standing up for what was right even when it was hard. If they plan to do it anyway, explain that they lose the game when they make unwise choices, and it's never wrong to do the right thing.

Baking Buddies

Life is filled with twists and turns that require careful planning, prayer, and consideration to help us learn to make wise choices. The Bible says, *"Trust in the LORD with all your heart; do not depend on your own understanding. Seek his will in all you do, and he will show you which path to take"* (Proverbs 3:5–6). We're making Choose Wisely Cinnamon Twists today because no matter what we face, we can trust in the Lord to guide us through every twist when we seek His wisdom as we make our choices.

CHOOSE WISELY
CINNAMON TWISTS

Ingredients

2 sheets of puff pastry (thawed to room temperature)
¼ cup butter, melted
1 cup granulated sugar
2 tsp. cinnamon

Icing

1 cup powdered sugar
1 tsp. pure vanilla extract
2-3 tbsp. milk (or milk alternative)

Directions

Preheat oven to 400°F.

Keep the two sheets of puff pastry on top of each other. On a piece of parchment paper, roll the pastry into a rectangle, approximately 12x10".

Brush the topside with the melted butter, being sure to cover it all.

In a small bowl, mix the sugar and cinnamon together, then sprinkle it over the entire surface over the butter. You can use your hands to gently pat it into the dough.

Fold the pastry in half the short way and roll it out slightly with your rolling pin to press it so it sticks together.

Brush the top with more butter and cover the surface with the sugar mixture again.

Use a pizza cutter or a knife to cut the pastry into 1" strips.

Twist each strip as tightly as you can.

Place the twisted strips on a baking sheet lined with parchment paper.

Bake for 15-20 minutes until golden and crispy. Then remove to a wire rack to allow them to cool.

In a small bowl, whisk together powdered sugar, vanilla, and 1 tbsp. milk. Add additional tablespoons of milk little by little as needed to reach the desired consistency for dipping. It should be thick, but not too thick to dip. You can pour into smaller individual bowls or leave it in that bowl for family dipping.

24

AGGRESSION

Stop being angry! Turn from your rage!
Do not lose your temper—it only leads to harm.
—Psalm 37:8

Our son Jordan went through a phase where he struggled to control his rage. He'd get so upset that he'd lash out physically in anger—biting, scratching, pinching, punching, or kicking. He'd especially lose his cool when his big sister did something he didn't like, or she attempted to "boss him around." He had these massive feelings inside his young body that he just didn't know how to control or appropriately express.

I wish I could tell you that it's simply a developmental issue and that all kids naturally grow out of their aggressive tendencies, but it isn't true. I witnessed this firsthand with the countless children and teens I worked with both in the counseling office and through the juvenile justice system. You only have to turn on the news to see violent actions perpetrated by adults as well.

Aggression needs to be addressed—and the sooner, the better. It's one thing when your adorable toddler is physically aggressive with you, but it's a whole other ballgame when your teen attacks someone.

A word of caution: regardless of your parenting and discipline styles or philosophies, I guarantee you that punishing aggressive behaviors with any form of aggression is counterproductive. If I hit or spank my child while telling them, "Don't hit your sister," I'm simply creating confusion and opening the door for resentment to burrow into their heart.

In order to effectively address aggressive behaviors in our children, we need to maintain control of our own emotions and impulses and master the art of de-escalation. This is a skill I was first taught in the social work field. I learned to maintain my composure, control my body language and tone of voice, and speak calmly without judgment or hostility so as not to escalate an already volatile situation. I'm not always perfect at this with my kiddos, even with all my training and experience, so don't be too hard on yourself when you fail—because you will fail at times. However, by modeling calm and nonviolent responses, we're showing our kids that it's possible and preferable to aggression. And when we fail, we can model how to take responsibility for our actions and clean up our own messes.

Parents' Prayer

Holy Spirit, help me control my own emotions and calmly approach my child when they're losing control of their anger. Fill our home with Your peace and protect us all. In Jesus's name I pray. Amen.

Teachable Moment

When we don't control our anger, our anger controls us. In Genesis 4, jealousy and anger cause Cain to kill his brother Abel. (Read this chapter with your kids or watch a kids' video of the story on the Internet.) Proverbs 29:11 (ERV) notes, *"Fools are quick to express their anger, but wise people are patient and control themselves."*

Physical activities such as exercise, playing sports, and going for a walk or a run can help to release the tension in our bodies when we're feeling upset. Others may include yelling out your frustration, talking it out, praying or praising God, and writing down your thoughts. Can you think of any other ideas? (Write them all down; create a visual for younger kids to help them quickly identify a healthier alternative when feeling angry.)

The Bible tells us, *"Don't repay evil for evil. Don't retaliate with insults when people insult you. Instead, pay them back with a blessing. That is what God has called you to do, and he will grant you his blessing"* (1 Peter 3:9). What are some ways we could bless people when we're feeling angry with them? Let's make a list.

Did you know that even as Jesus was about to be led to His death, He modeled this for us? His disciple Peter drew his sword and tried to defend Jesus with violence, cutting off the ear of one of the high priest's men. (See Matthew 26:50–52; Mark 14:47; Luke 22:49–50; John 18:10–11.) Let's read these passages of Scripture to see how Jesus responded to Peter's aggression. Jesus didn't want Peter to hurt others. In fact, Jesus even healed the man's ear. The Bible teaches us:

> But now is the time to get rid of anger, rage, malicious behavior, slander, and dirty language. Don't lie to each other, for you have stripped off your old sinful nature and all its wicked deeds. Put on your new nature, and be renewed as you learn to know your Creator and become like him. (Colossians 3:8–10)

When we ask Jesus to be our Lord and Savior, we become new creations. And the more time we spend with Jesus, the more we become like Him. But we can't do it on our own. We need to pray and ask the Holy Spirit to help us. Let's do that now by praying aloud together.

For older kids, you could also study famous people in history who sought to solve problems in the way modeled by Jesus, such as the Rev. Martin Luther King Jr. and Mother Teresa.

Conversation Connection

> » What seems to set off your anger the most? Why do you think that is?

» Can you think of a time where you wanted to hurt someone, but you didn't? How were you able to control yourself in that moment?

» What are some calming techniques we could use to calm ourselves down when we feel like we are losing control of our temper?

» How can I help you when you're feeling really upset? What do you need from me?

Family Fun

Instead of being aggressive, we should learn to cooperate with those who frustrate us. Psalm 34:14 says, *"Turn away from evil and do good. Search for peace, and work to maintain it."* Today we're going to have fun working together to accomplish our goal by having three-legged races. Use a bandana, large sock, or a pillowcase to wrap around the legs of two people—one person's left leg and the other's right leg. This should be tight enough to keep the legs close but not too tight to cut off circulation. Choose start and finish lines. Depending on the ages of your children, you can have variations of this game, like blindfolding one player or both, walking backward, keeping a balloon between the two without dropping or popping it, having one player face forward while the other faces backward, or making it an obstacle course that requires actions such as crawling under a table or hopping over an object. Have fun and work together; practice keeping your cool when frustrated and using your words to communicate instead of aggression.

Baking Buddies

The Bible says, *"You're blessed when you can show people how to cooperate instead of compete or fight. That's when you discover who you really are, and your place in God's family"* (Matthew 5:9 MSG). As children of God, we want to be peacemakers and dump aggressive behaviors, so today we're making Peaceful Peach—Dump the Aggression—Cake.

PEACEFUL PEACH—
DUMP THE AGGRESSION—CAKE

Ingredients

2 (16 oz.) cans of peaches in heavy syrup (or juice)
1 box of yellow cake mix*
½ cup butter
½ tsp. ground cinnamon
*You can also make the recipe with fresh or frozen peaches if you prefer.
You'll just need to toss together about 2-3 cups of sliced peaches, ½ cup
sugar, and 1 tbsp. cornstarch—and be sure to spray or butter the cake
pan first. Then follow the rest of the recipe.*
**You can also use a gluten-free cake mix.*

Directions

Preheat oven to 375°F.

Empty the cans of peaches into a 13x9" baking pan into an even layer.

Pour the dry cake mix evenly over the top of the peaches and use a
spatula to press down firmly.

Cut the stick of butter into small slices and scatter it over the top of
the cake mix.

Sprinkle the cinnamon over the top.

Bake approximately 40-45 minutes, until the top of the cake is golden
brown.

Allow it to cool some before serving.

Feel free to add some ice cream or whipped cream on top.

25

LACK OF INTEGRITY/DECEIT

People with integrity walk safely,
but those who follow crooked paths will be exposed.
—Proverbs 10:9

Integrity means you do the right thing even when no one is looking. You are a person of your word. Trustworthy. This doesn't come naturally to us, so we all face situations in life that challenge our integrity. How will we respond?

Even our young kids wrestle with this. When push comes to shove, will they practice integrity or dishonesty? I don't know about your kids, but mine have definitely fallen prey to deceit.

I'll never forget the first time our daughter cut her hair. She couldn't have been older than four, yet she knew what she was doing was wrong. She not only cut her hair, she dumped it in the toilet to hide the evidence! She was shocked when I discovered her deception and admitted she had attempted to conceal it.

Her deceitful ways continued with behaviors like shoving things under her bed or in her closet when asked to clean her room, blaming her brother instead of taking responsibility, and telling tall tales to try to get out of trouble.

It's easy to slip into deceitful practices as we experience pressure in our daily lives, but we are called to walk in integrity. And if we want our children to follow, we must lead with integrity.

The righteous man who walks in integrity and lives life in accord with his [godly] beliefs—how blessed [happy and spiritually secure] are his children after him [who have his example to follow].

(Proverbs 20:7 AMP)

Parents' Prayer

Jesus, help me to lead with integrity and guide my children to walk in the path of integrity all the days of their lives. Amen.

Teachable Moment

Select one of your child's favorite candies or treats. Put ten pieces of candy in a bowl and tell your child they can have one piece of candy while you leave the room briefly to do something. When you come back, ask how many pieces of candy they had. Then count to confirm. If they only ate one, praise them for demonstrating integrity by doing the right thing even when you weren't looking. If they ate more than one, tell them that they passed up an opportunity to act honorably instead of deceitfully.

Explain that the Bible teaches us, "*The integrity of the honest keeps them on track; the deviousness of crooks brings them to ruin*" (Proverbs 11:3 MSG). Integrity means doing the right thing and being a person of your word no matter what. Because Jesus had integrity, He treated others well, did what He said He would do, and was honest and trustworthy.

We're going to study what the Bible says about integrity to help us overcome the temptation to do what's wrong instead of what's right. Have your older kids search and write out verses about integrity. (See, for example, Psalms 7:8; 25:21; 41:12; Proverbs 10:9; 11:3; 19:1; 20:7; 28:6; 28:18; 2 Corinthians 8:21.) For younger kids, choose one or two verses for them to copy and memorize. They can keep it simple or decorate it like a poster to hang on the wall.

Conversation Connection

>> What does it mean to be a person of integrity?

>> Can you think of a time where you chose to do what was wrong instead of right? How did you feel afterward?

>> Why do you think integrity is important?

>> What can you do to be more honorable?

Family Fun

Explain to your kids that when we're people of integrity, we have nothing to hide. Instead, we seek the truth and seek to always do what we know is right. The Bible tells us, *"Everything that is hidden will become clear. Every thing that is hidden will be made known, and everyone will see it"* (Luke 8:17 ERV). Now play the classic game of hide and seek. One person is the truth seeker (finder) and the others hide somewhere until they are found. Repeat as many times as you'd like.

Baking Buddies

We want to be people of integrity and look at ourselves and others as followers of Jesus. Second Corinthians 5:16–17 says, *"So we have stopped evaluating others from a human point of view. At one time we thought of Christ merely from a human point of view. How differently we know him now! This means that anyone who belongs to Christ has become a new person. The old life is gone; a new life has begun!"* Today we're making Is It Really a Cake Cookie? to remind us that Jesus takes our lives and makes us brand new in Him when we surrender our lives to Him.

IS IT REALLY A CAKE COOKIE?

Ingredients

1 box white cake mix (or flavor of choice)

¼ cup all-purpose flour (if using a gluten-free cake mix that has 17 oz. instead of the traditional 15 oz., you don't need the extra flour)

2 large eggs

½ cup vegetable oil

1 cup of mix-ins (mini chocolate chips, sprinkles, candies, etc.)

Directions

Preheat oven to 350°F and line a baking sheet with parchment paper. Set aside.

In a large bowl (or the bowl of your stand mixer), mix together cake mix, eggs, and oil until smooth.

Add in mix-ins and stir to combine.

Use a cookie scoop to scoop 2" cookies onto your baking sheet approximately 2" apart.

Bake 8-10 minutes, or until the edges are lightly golden.

SECTION THREE

RELATIONAL CHALLENGES

26

SIBLING RIVALRY

Get rid of all bitterness, rage, anger, harsh words,
and slander, as well as all types of evil behavior.
Instead, be kind to each other, tenderhearted, forgiving one another,
just as God through Christ has forgiven you.
—Ephesians 4:31–32

I'm not sure when or how it happened, but suddenly, my children, who were once the best of friends, began clashing like the worst enemies. They broke into constant bickering and competition, along with comparing, complaining, and fighting. At best, they were frenemies.

It's like they forgot who they were—family, best friends, children of God, brother and sister. The truth is, the closer we are in our heart-to-heart relationships, the more we tend to hurt each other. So what can we do about it?

Sometimes, we simply need a little distance to gain perspective. In our situation, we recognized the time for room-sharing had come to an end. They needed their own spaces so they could have more control in their day-to-day activities, a place where they could escape when overwhelmed or frustrated. Thankfully, this helped—a lot!

Even so, sibling rivalry rears its ugly head from time to time. It's a natural part of family life. When it does, we try to spend time out of the house with each child individually. We reconnect and explore what's at the root of their frustration. We help our kids pray for one another and practice empathy, the art of putting oneself in someone else's shoes. This carries us a long way the next time sibling rivalry pops up.

Sibling relationships are incredibly special. They create countless opportunities to model biblical behavior and learn invaluable life skills. They are a gift to be cherished, and it's our responsibility as parents to help our children recognize this and respond accordingly.

Parents' Prayer

Heavenly Father, thank You for the blessing of my children. Thank You for the life lessons they learn from one another and the opportunities You give us to grow together and become more like Your Son. Help us to be patient and loving with each other as You reveal any heart issues that hinder our relationships. In Jesus's name I pray. Amen.

Teachable Moment

The Bible teaches us, "*Love each other with genuine affection, and take delight in honoring each other*" (Romans 12:10). It also warns, "*Don't be selfish; don't try to impress others. Be humble, thinking of others as better than yourselves*" (Philippians 2:3). In another translation, the last part of this verse reads, "*in lowliness of mind let each esteem others better than himself*" (NKJV).

As a family, we want to celebrate each other's strengths and differences, keeping in mind that we *are* on the same team. A win for one is a win for all, just as a loss for one is a loss for all. We're going to make name signs that include some of the best traits each of us has. Use your first names as an acronym for all of the attributes you love about each other. For example, for *KATIE*, I might have: *Kind, Attentive, Thoughtful, Inspirational,*

Encouraging. Decorate and hang your signs, and then come up with one together for your last name. Frame it somewhere prominent to remind yourselves that you are a team and not rivals.

Conversation Connection

» What do you love most about your siblings?

» What makes you unique?

» What does it mean to be a team?

» Did you know God created our family as a team and our family is part of Jesus's team? Together, we get to help build the kingdom of God.

» How can we make our team stronger?

Family Fun

We aren't rivals; we're a team, and teams win or lose together. Create a team name for your family and design a team logo together. You could also do a team-building activity. Using plastic straws and masking tape, have each person try to build the tallest tower by themselves for three minutes. Next, try again with someone attempting to sabotage your efforts. Finally, work together as a family to build one tall tower together. Emphasize the fact that, "We are better together, and we're on the same team!" We are all part of the body of Christ.

God did this so that our body would not be divided. God wanted the different parts to care the same for each other. If one part of the body suffers, then all the other parts suffer with it. Or if one part is honored, then all the other parts share its honor. All of you together are the body of Christ. Each one of you is a part of that body.

(1 Corinthians 12:25–27 ERV)

Baking Buddies

Life is messy, and our feelings sometimes muddy the waters. But at the end of the day, we don't want to forget that our siblings will be with us through the good and the bad. They are our forever friends. *"Friends love through all kinds of weather, and families stick together in all kinds of trouble"* (Proverbs 17:17 MSG). Today we're making Muddy Buddies for Life to remind us that siblings stick together through it all.

MUDDY BUDDIES FOR LIFE
(GLUTEN-FREE)

Ingredients

3 cups Rice Chex cereal

3 cups Corn Chex cereal

3 cups Chocolate Chex cereal

(You can use any combination of cereal you want to equal 9 cups)

1 cup semisweet chocolate chips

½ cup creamy (or crunchy) peanut butter (or other nut butter)

¼ cup butter

1 tsp. vanilla extract

1 ½ cups powdered sugar

Directions

Pour cereal into large bowl and set aside.

Using a 1-quart microwavable bowl, microwave the chocolate chips, peanut butter, and butter on high for one minute. Stir and microwave for an additional 30 seconds. Stir until smooth. Add in vanilla and stir.

Pour mixture over cereal, stirring with rubber spatula until evenly coated.

Pour coated mixture into gallon resealable freezer bag.

Add powdered sugar to bag and seal tightly. Shake bag until cereal is well-coated.

Place waxed paper on a sheet tray and empty bag onto tray to cool. Then enjoy.

27

PEER PRESSURE

Walk with the wise and become wise;
associate with fools and get in trouble.
—Proverbs 13:20

The desire to belong and be accepted flows deeply through each of us, which is why peer pressure can be so challenging. We desperately want to fit in, even though we were created to stand out. Jesus calls us to be *"the salt of the earth"* and *"the light of the world"* (Matthew 5:13–14), but we can't be either of those when we're trying to be like everyone else.

As parents, we often think that the peer pressure our kids face involves breaking the law or committing terrible sins. But typically, it's more minor offenses—like listening to music, watching a show, or playing a game that we have forbidden. It's those little compromises that cultivate rebellion in our children's hearts and minds.

Both of our kids have experienced this type of peer pressure many times in their short lives, with friends wanting them to watch or play something they know that we oppose. Our children have learned how to communicate their boundaries and offer alternatives. They also aren't afraid to walk away and come to us if their friends won't respect their boundaries. It's taken a lot of conversations, and I'm sure we'll continue to discuss these types of things as they mature and face new challenges, but we're growing through it.

Sometimes peer pressure is easy to navigate, but more often than not, it's a complex issue that requires patience, open communication, and empathy from us as parents. We can't pretend it's always black and white when it's really gray. What's acceptable for one child may not be acceptable for another.

What one Christian family says is okay may be something you forbid and vice versa. We don't want to inadvertently teach our children that *our* convictions need to be everyone else's convictions. We need to take the time to process with our kids and explore alternatives and solutions to challenging situations, rather than adhering to a "just say no" philosophy. Our kids need to know how to reason, make wise decisions, pray, search the Scriptures, and allow the Holy Spirit to guide their choices.

Parents' Prayer

God, give me wisdom and patience to help my children recognize and resist peer pressure. Strengthen our relationship and help us communicate well so we can walk through life's challenges together. In Jesus's name I pray. Amen.

Teachable Moment

There are a lot of examples in the Bible of people struggling with peer pressure. Many gave in to it and experienced significant consequences as a result. But others stood firm and made the right choices, even when it was hard.

Saul gave in to peer pressure and offered a sacrifice to God instead of waiting for Samuel to arrive because his army was becoming fearful and abandoning him. (See 1 Samuel 13:6–14.) Saul not only lost his kingdom but ruined his family's chances of ruling forever.

Aaron gave in to peer pressure too. While Moses was up on the mountain talking with God, the Israelites became restless. (See Exodus 32.) They begged Aaron to create a god for them, so he formed a golden calf. God sent a plague, and many lost their lives.

David also experienced a lot of peer pressure before he was crowned king. Then-king Saul was hunting David and trying to kill him. David's friends encouraged him to kill Saul, but David refused to harm God's anointed one. David could have done it once while Saul was asleep, but not only did he reject his friends' advice, he didn't permit them to kill Saul either. Instead, he left a sword in his cloak so Saul would know that David could have killed him but chose not to. (See 1 Samuel 24, 26.) Later, when Saul died, instead of rejoicing, David ordered the death of the Amalekite who claimed to have killed Saul. (See 1 Samuel 31:4–6; 2 Samuel 1:14–15.)

Talk to your kids about ways to handle peer pressure and then either role-play them or draw them out like a comic book scene. Options for dealing with peer pressure can include simply saying "no," walking away, and sharing our boundaries, such as telling the other person, "I am not allowed to watch/do/say that" or "I don't want to ___." Make sure your kids know that they can call you anytime, and you will bring them home if they're in a bad situation.

Conversation Connection

» What does peer pressure mean?

» Can you think of a time when you gave in to peer pressure? What happened?

» Can you remember a time when people tried to get you to do something you knew was wrong but you didn't give in to the peer pressure? How were you able to do that?

» What are some things you can do when you face peer pressure?

Family Fun

In life, we've got to be diligent about avoiding the traps of peer pressure. The Bible warns us, *"Don't take the path of the wicked; don't follow those who do evil. Stay away from that path; don't even go near it. Turn around and go another way"* (Proverbs 4:14–15 ERV). Today we're going to play a game of Sharks and Minnows. One person is the shark to start and stands in the middle of the yard or room. Minnows line up on one end and try to get safely to the other end without being tagged by the shark. If they're tagged by the shark, they stop where they're at and become sharks, trying to tag the other minnows attempting to cross back and forth. The last minnow to avoid capture wins.

Baking Buddies

There's an old saying, "If you play with fire, you're going to get burned." The friends we surround ourselves with matter. When we allow ourselves to remain in unhealthy situations, we're more likely to give in to temptation and make a poor choice. Today we're making Don't Get Burnt by Peer Pressure S'mores Bars to remind us that when we face the refining fire of God, we don't want to give in to the pressures around us, but stand firm on the truth and do what's right.

> *God blesses those who patiently endure testing and temptation. Afterward they will receive the crown of life that God has promised to those who love him. And remember, when you are being tempted, do not say, "God is tempting me." God is never tempted to do wrong, and he never tempts anyone else.* (James 1:12–13)

DON'T GET BURNT BY PEER PRESSURE S'MORES BARS

Ingredients

½ cup unsalted butter (1 stick), melted
1 cup light brown sugar (packed)
1 large egg
1 tbsp. vanilla extract
¾ cup all-purpose flour
5 full graham crackers
1 cup mini marshmallows
1 cup semisweet chocolate chips

Directions

Preheat oven to 350ºF and line an 8x8" baking pan with aluminum foil, leaving an extra inch or two hanging over two sides so you can use them as handles for easy removal. Spray the top of the foil inside the pan with cooking spray and set aside.

In a large, microwave-safe bowl, melt the butter (30-60 seconds).

Allow the butter to cool for a minute before adding the brown sugar, vanilla, and egg (so you don't scramble the egg). Whisk until combined.

Add the flour, stirring just until incorporated, so as not to overmix.

Break the graham crackers into large chunks and add them (and the crumbs) into the mix along with the chocolate chips and marshmallows. Fold them into the batter to combine.

Pour batter into the prepared pan and use a spatula to gently press and spread the mixture.

Bake for 20-25 minutes, until the edges are set and the center has firmed up. The marshmallows should look a bit golden. (If you don't like chewy centers, bake a little longer).

Let the bars cool in the pan for at least a half hour before removing from pan and slicing into squares. Serve and enjoy.

18

BULLYING

Forget about the wrong things people do to you. Don't try to get even.
Love your neighbor as yourself. I am the LORD.
—Leviticus 19:18 (ERV)

Whether your child is the one being bullied or the one doing the bullying, it's a common issue that touches most families these days, especially with social media. Bullying may not seem like a major deal, but I can assure you, it's led to the loss of countless young lives and the destruction of so many more.

I grew up with the adage, "Sticks and stones may break your bones, but words will never hurt you." However, I think we've all learned how wrong that is. Bones heal, but harsh words leave scars. That's why bullying others with our words, whether spoken or typed, can lead to irreparable harm.

At the age of ten, our daughter has already received a fair amount of bullying. At a homeschool group, some kids decided it would be fun to exclude her and run away from her anytime she came near them. Then they began to lie about her and call her hurtful names. It was a difficult season for all of us, and we had to walk her through how to set healthy boundaries, communicate her needs, and stand up for herself, while also teaching her how not to let others' words and actions define who she truly is.

The following year, she was accused of bullying herself. She had seen a young man act aggressively toward a girl, so she began avoiding him within the group. It wasn't until weeks later when a parent finally brought the situation up that we were able to bring the kids together and work through the issue.

Our kids need our support in navigating these tricky situations, and they happen all around us, even for those of us who homeschool. At first, I felt upset that Kendra was exposed to bullying at such a young age. Now, however, I realize what a blessing it is that I was there when it happened. It created opportunities to teach her lifelong skills and begin a conversation that we continue to build upon.

It's important for us to teach our children to be accountable not just for what they say and do in person, but how they steward social media as well. Most social media apps have an age restriction because even their creators realize they aren't appropriate for young hearts and minds. Some adults are unable to appropriately manage themselves and their relationships on social media, so how can we expect our children and teens to do any better?

Our kids need to understand how their words and actions impact the lives of others. And they need to be held responsible for those choices. As parents, it's our responsibility to help them understand the dangers of social media, including how to identify healthy versus unhealthy interactions—and what to do about them. We want to use caution and not expose them to social media too early, before they're mature enough to handle it.

We need to equip our kids with the tools to take responsibility for themselves and set healthy boundaries with others. They need to understand the permanency of what they post on the Internet, even if they quickly delete something. And they need a solid foundation in Christ so they aren't swayed by the ebb and flow of bullying so rampant on the Internet right now. Regardless of what age we allow our children to get online, we must make sure we're providing proper education and support to help them navigate the challenges ahead.

Parents' Prayer

Holy Spirit, give me wisdom and discernment to navigate these issues of bullying with my kids. Give me the words to speak and strategies for overcoming this struggle. In Jesus's name I pray. Amen.

Teachable Moment

The Bible instructs us, "*Do to others whatever you would like them to do to you. This is the essence of all that is taught in the law and the prophets*" (Matthew 7:12). Some call it the Golden Rule. Jesus teaches us the importance of loving others and treating them well—even our enemies. Our Lord said, "*You have heard that it was said, 'Love your neighbor and hate your enemy.' But I tell you, love your enemies. Pray for those who treat you badly*" (Matthew 5:43–44 ERV).

I was always taught that *hurting people hurt people*. If we find ourselves hurting others, there's probably some hurt inside us that we need to heal. And if other people are hurting us, we can remember that they are obviously hurting and going through something, which can help us to show compassion to them even when they treat us badly.

In the Bible, Joseph was bullied by his brothers. They were so jealous of him that they thought about killing him. But instead, they sold Joseph into slavery, and he was shipped off to another land. (See Genesis 37.)

Joseph went through many very hard years as a result of his brothers' evil behavior. He even spent several years in prison when he hadn't done anything wrong. But when Joseph got out of prison and became a powerful ruler, he forgave his brothers and blessed them. Love always wins.

Depending on the ages of your children, read the story of Joseph in Genesis 37–50, find the story in a children's Bible, or watch a video about his life. Discuss how Joseph was able to keep his heart pure and refrain from seeking revenge against his brothers. Talk about why they hurt Joseph (jealousy, bitterness, etc.) and what they could have done about those feelings instead.

Conversation Connection

> » How would you define or explain bullying?

> » What thoughts or feelings do you think lead to bullying behaviors? Why?

> » What can you do if you're being bullied?

> » If you feel like hurting someone else, what can you do instead?

Family Fun

Forget about the wrong things people do to you. Don't try to get even. Love your neighbor as yourself. I am the LORD.

(Leviticus 19:18 ERV)

Bullies are likes bulls in a china shop; they cause destruction wherever they go. We don't want to be like that, and we want to learn how to avoid a bully's path of destruction. So today, we're going to play a game of No Bulls Family Bowling. You can go to a bowling alley or simply set up a homemade game in your home or driveway. Choose a ball and set up ten plastic cups, bottles, or some other tall, lightweight, nonbreakable items in a pyramid. Then take turns rolling the ball to try to knock them down.

Baking Buddies

The Bible teaches us that there's no room for bullying in this world. *"But to you who are willing to listen, I say, love your enemies! Do good to those who hate you. Bless those who curse you. Pray for those who hurt you"* (Luke 6:27–28). Today we're making No-Bully Wins Bread Pudding to remind us that love covers a multitude of sins, just as our pure vanilla sauce will cover our bowl of bread pudding. Bullying tears people apart and only the love of God can bring us together.

NO-BULLY WINS BREAD PUDDING

Ingredients

2 ½ cups heavy cream (or milk for a lighter dessert)
1 ½ cups granulated sugar
¼ cup butter (melted)
3 eggs (beaten)
2 tbsp. brown sugar
½ tsp. ground cinnamon
Loaf of thick, sturdy bread (like brioche or challah; 10 slices if already sliced)
· 1 cup raisins (optional but highly recommended)

Sauce

1 ¼ cups whole milk
½ cup brown sugar
2 tbsp. melted butter
1 egg
1 tbsp. all-purpose flour
1 pinch ground cinnamon
1 pinch salt
1 tbsp. pure vanilla extract

Directions

Preheat oven to 375°F and grease a 3-quart baking dish. Set aside.

Chop bread into 1" cubes. (For slices of bread, I cut them in half lengthwise and then into 1" cubes.) *I recommend parents do this step for safety, or you can simply have the kids rip the bread into large chunks if you wish and talk about how bullying tears people apart.*

In a small, microwave safe bowl, melt butter. Then allow it to cool slightly.

In a separate small bowl, beat the three eggs together.

In a large mixing bowl, whisk together cream or milk, sugar, melted butter, eggs, brown sugar, and cinnamon.

Gently stir the bread cubes (and raisins) into the mixture to coat evenly.

Carefully spoon the mixture into your prepared baking dish.

Bake for 30 minutes. An adult should carefully cover the dish with a piece of foil to prevent excessive browning. (*Cut slits into the foil before placing it on the dish if you want the pudding to be a little dryer*).

Bake for an additional 20-35 minutes until it reaches your desired consistency (should have absorbed all the liquid and be golden, but you can decide how crispy or moist you like it).

Allow it to cool for 10 minutes before serving as you make the sauce.

To make the vanilla sauce, combine milk, brown sugar, butter, egg, flour, salt, and cinnamon in a saucepan and cook over medium heat—whisking constantly for 10-12 minutes, or until the sauce thickens and coats the back of your spoon.

Remove sauce from heat and stir in vanilla extract.

You can pour the sauce directly over the bread pudding or serve it in a side dish.

29

BACK TALKING/ARGUING

Again I say, don't get involved in foolish, ignorant arguments that only start fights. A servant of the Lord must not quarrel but must be kind to everyone, be able to teach, and be patient with difficult people.
—2 Timothy 2:23–24

Our daughter Kendra is especially skilled in the art of arguing. Along with her deep sense of right and wrong is a strong desire to understand (and agree with) everything, even things that don't concern her. This has proven to be especially challenging to navigate as her parents.

We recognize the leadership qualities and passion God has placed within our daughter. We want her to question and seek to understand the world around her because we believe that's how she'll change the world for the better. However, we also recognize that she needs to learn the importance of honoring her parents and other authorities that God has placed in her life, as well as life lessons such as knowing when to fight for justice and when to be silent or disagree appropriately.

As parents, it's been a balancing act to navigate these challenges while equipping our children for their future. We want to help them mature in those traits that may drive us crazy without squashing them completely. Why? Because we believe God placed them there for a purpose, and we want to set our children up to be the best version of themselves they possibly can be. We want them to embrace their uniqueness—and that includes attributes the world may or may not always value and appreciate.

James and I often joke about Kendra's shrewd negotiating skills and her ability to persuasively argue her points. I'm not yet sure how God will utilize those traits to help her fulfill her purpose on this earth, but I know *He* knows. And it's our job to help her hone those skills in a way that honors both us and God—not strip her of them completely in an attempt to force submission. This type of parenting requires prayer and wisdom. We don't always get it right, but we're always looking to grow and extend the same grace to our kids that God extends to us.

Parents' Prayer

Heavenly Father, thank You for Your patience with me. Grant me wisdom as I address my child's back talking and arguing. Help me to nurture the traits You have placed in them for a purpose and experience freedom from those things that aren't of You. In Jesus's name I pray. Amen.

Teachable Moment

The first commandment with a promise appears in Exodus 20:12 (AMP): "*Honor (respect, obey, care for) your father and your mother, so that your days may be prolonged in the land the LORD your God gives you.*" The Bible also says, "*Children, obey your parents in all things, for this is well pleasing to the Lord*" (Colossians 3:20 NKJV). There's a difference between arguing or back talking and pleading your case. "*People who refuse to argue deserve respect. Any fool can start an argument*" (Proverbs 20:3 ERV). Can you think of a time when it would be appropriate to plead your case (court of law, debate, discussion)?

We see a number of instances in the Bible in which people pleaded their cases with God, for example:

» Abraham asked God to spare Sodom and Gomorrah in Genesis 18:22–33.

» Moses begged God not to destroy the Israelites after they convinced his brother Aaron to make a golden calf for them to worship in Exodus 32:9–14.

» Hezekiah prayed that God would let him live longer in 2 Kings 20:1–11.

Here, we see that Moses and Abraham intervened on behalf of others, while Hezekiah was only looking out for himself. And although God granted the request for the sake of His honor and King David's faithfulness, Hezekiah made a foolish mistake that proved costly for both him and his sons. (See verses 12–19.)

Take the time to set up expectations for the right and wrong ways to disagree and write them out as family guidelines, along with consequences for not following them. Then role-play how to do it correctly. A good book to help younger children with this concept is *I Just Don't Like the Sound of No!* by Julie Cook.[4]

Conversation Connection

» What do you think is wrong with arguing?

» Can you think of a time when arguing with someone is the right thing to do? How could you do it appropriately?

» How can you keep from arguing or back talking when you feel upset?

---

4. Julie Cook, *I Just Don't Like the Sound of No! My Story About Accepting No for an Answer and Disagreeing the Right Way* (Boys Town, NE: Boys Town Press, 2011).

Family Fun

There are rules and expectations for every aspect of life. The Bible provides us with guidelines that help us honor God and bless others with our lives. Paul writes:

> *Remind the believers to submit to the government and its officers. They should be obedient, always ready to do what is good. They must not slander anyone and must avoid quarreling. Instead, they should be gentle and show true humility to everyone.*   (Titus 3:1–2)

Today, we're going to have fun pleading our case before the judge, king, or queen in the right way, with a mock trial. Take turns being the one making the ruling and the one pleading their case. You can make up scenarios or take this opportunity to allow your children to attempt to persuade you of the merits of something they want to do or have. Either way, make it fun and model effective debate skills. Explain that there's a time and a place for discussion, and a time to accept and trust what your parent, boss, judge, or leader says.

Baking Buddies

Proverbs 13:10 (ERV) warns us that *"Pride causes arguments, but those who listen to others are wise."* Today we're making kNOT Arguing Pretzels to remind us to be flexible and not tie ourselves up in knots with arguments, but instead to listen and be wise.

KNOT ARGUING PRETZELS

Ingredients

1 ½ cups warm (not hot) water
1 tbsp. sugar
2 tsp. salt
1 pkg. active dry yeast
4 ½ cups all-purpose flour
4 tbsp. butter, melted
10 cups water
⅔ cup baking soda
1 large egg yolk
1 tbsp. water
Large coarse salt or cinnamon/sugar for tops
Vegetable oil (for the bowl and pans)

Directions

In the bowl of your stand mixer, combine the warm water (1 ½ cups) with the sugar and salt. Sprinkle the yeast packet over the top and let it sit for approximately 5 minutes, or until it begins to foam.

Add in the flour and butter. Use the dough hook attachment and mix on low until combined. Then increase speed to medium to knead the dough until it's smooth and pulls away from the side of the bowl (approximately 4-5 minutes).

Use another large bowl and oil it with vegetable oil until it is fully coated. Place the dough in the bowl and cover with plastic wrap or a towel. Allow it to sit for about an hour in a warm place (until it doubles in size).

Preheat oven to 450°F and line two half-sheet pans with parchment paper. Lightly brush the parchment paper with oil and set aside.

In a large saucepan, boil the 10 cups of water and the baking soda.

Lightly oil your counter or work surface and turn your dough out onto it. Divide the dough into 8 even pieces using a bench scraper or knife.

Roll out each piece into a long rope, approximately 22-24 inches. Make a U-shape, holding the two ends of the rope. Cross the ends over each other twice and press them into the middle of the U-shape to make your pretzel. You can also have fun with this and make any shape you desire, such as a heart, star, or animal face.

An *adult* should carefully place each pretzel, one at a time, in the boiling water for 30 seconds. Use a large flat spatula to carefully remove the pretzel from the water and place it on the sheet pan, leaving approximately 2 inches between pretzels. Continue until all the pretzels are on the sheet pans (4 per pan).

In a small bowl, beat the egg yolk and 1 tbsp. water.

Brush the yolk mixture on the top of each pretzel and sprinkle with coarse salt. *If you want cinnamon/sugar pretzels, wait until after they are cooked, then brush with melted butter and sprinkle cinnamon/sugar mixture on top.*

Bake for 12-14 minutes, until pretzels are golden brown.

Transfer to wire racks and allow to cool for five minutes prior to serving.

30

TEASING

The tongue can bring death or life;
those who love to talk will reap the consequences.
—Proverbs 18:21

Teasing tends to stick with us long after the words have been spoken. I imagine you can still recall teasing that you endured as a child. I know I can. There was the boy in school who made fun of the hair on the back of my neck, which kept me from wearing my hair up for many years… and made me feel insecure when I finally did pull it up.

Even my sweet husband once commented that I looked like a boy with my hair in a ponytail. And my brothers called me and my sisters fat for as long as I can remember. The list could go on, but you get my point. Teasing is toxic and slowly poisons us from the inside out if we aren't careful.

Some people tend to tease as a form of endearment. James struggles with this at times. And whereas our son Jordan doesn't seem fazed by it, our daughter Kendra is another story. Every word leaves a mark, burrowing deep in her heart.

One day, James made another seemingly innocent comment regarding Kendra's teeth. Finally, she'd had enough—and explained how her father's remarks hurt her and made her feel bad. Of course, James felt terrible, so he apologized profusely and promised not to mention anything about her teeth again. What he thought were endearing words were actually a form of teasing that made Kendra feel insecure.

We all learned a lesson that day, and it's a great reminder of the power of our words. Whether our kids are on the giving or receiving end of teasing, I think we'd all agree that it's an issue we need to address. We want to teach our kids to be accountable for every word they speak so they don't cause harm to others. As parents, we want to provide our kids with the tools to remain firmly rooted in their identity in Christ, so they don't get knocked around by the thoughtless words of others or allow themselves to be defined by anything other than Jesus.

Parents' Prayer

God, forgive me for any careless words I've spoken that have hurt my family or others. Put a guard over my mouth and help me to speak words of life in every situation. Heal any wounds from words that my child has and help them to learn to speak life as well. In Jesus's name I pray. Amen.

Teachable Moment

Just as damaging as a madman shooting a deadly weapon is someone who lies to a friend and then says, "I was only joking."
(Proverbs 26:18–19)

Speak without thinking, and your words can cut like a knife. Be wise, and your words can heal. (Proverbs 12:18 ERV)

We may not see our words after we've spoken them, but they leave an imprint on those who hear them. We can choose whether our words bring life, hope, and encouragement, or bruises and scars.

If your child is the one doing the teasing, write the name of the person they've been teasing on a piece of paper. Have them use scissors or a pencil to stab holes into the paper, or simply have them crumple it up into a small ball. Then ask them to make the paper whole again or return it to its original version. (They can't.) Explain that we cannot take back our words once we've said them, and each hurtful word leaves a scar on the other person. We should always think before we speak. Psalm 141:3 (AMP) says, "*Set a guard, O LORD, over my mouth; keep watch over the door of my lips [to keep me from speaking thoughtlessly].*" We can make that our prayer as we work to choose our words more carefully.

If your child is being teased, explain that while words are hurtful, God can heal us from the pain inflicted by others. Psalm 147:3–4 (AMP) says, "*He heals the brokenhearted and binds up their wounds [healing their pain and comforting their sorrow]. He counts the number of the stars; He calls them all by their names.*" The Bible teaches us that God uniquely formed each of us.

You made all the delicate, inner parts of my body and knit me together in my mother's womb. Thank you for making me so wonderfully complex! Your workmanship is marvelous—how well I know it. You watched me as I was being formed in utter seclusion, as I was woven together in the dark of the womb. You saw me before I was born. Every day of my life was recorded in your book. Every moment was laid out before a single day had passed. How precious are your thoughts about me, O God. They cannot be numbered! I can't even count them; they outnumber the grains of sand! And when I wake up, you are still with me! (Psalm 139:13–18)

Not only did God uniquely create you, He loves you completely and cares deeply about even the smallest details of your life. You can go to Him in prayer with anything. Jesus tells us:

When birds are sold, five small birds cost only two pennies. But God does not forget any of them. Yes, God even knows how many hairs you have on your head. Don't be afraid. You are worth much more than many birds. (Luke 12:6–7 ERV)

We are not who the world says we are; we are who God, our Creator and loving heavenly Father, says we are. Let's spend some time in God's Word, searching for Scriptures on this matter. Create an "I Am…" poster or journal and list out the truths from God's Word to combat the lies others have spoken over your child. You can help to write the words and your child can draw pictures if they are younger.

When they're feeling discouraged, have them speak these truths aloud in front of the mirror:

» I am loved (John 3:16; Romans 8:35–39; 1 John 4:19).

» I am safe and protected (Psalms 32:7; 46:1; 62:2; 2 Thessalonians 3:3).

» I am free (John 8:36; 2 Corinthians 3:17; Galatians 5:1).

» I am righteous (2 Corinthians 5:21; 1 John 3:7).

» I am beautiful and made in God's image (Genesis 1:27; Psalm 139:14; Song of Solomon 4:7; Ephesians 2:10).

» I am Christ's friend (John 15:12–15).

» I am a child of God (John 1:12; Romans 8:16; Galatians 3:26; 1 John 3:1).

Conversation Connection

» What does it mean to tease someone?

» Can you think of a time someone teased you? How did it feel?

» Can you think of a time you teased someone else? How do you think they felt?

» Why do our words matter? How can we use our words to give life to others?

Family Fun

Today, we're going to play "I Love You Because..." Choose one person to sit in the "hot seat," a chair in the middle of everyone. The others take turns saying, "I love you because..." and then share all the things they love and appreciate about that person. You may want to create an audio recording of what everyone says or have one person write them all down. Or you can have each person take an index card and write out what they love about each person.

Explain that today we're going to practice building each other up and encouraging each other by sharing all the things we love about them. The Bible says, *"So encourage each other and build each other up, just as you are already doing"* (1 Thessalonians 5:11).

Baking Buddies

Since we're learning to stop and think before we speak, today we're making Count to Tres Leches Cake to remind us of this three-step process to prevent us from teasing others with hurtful words. *Tres leches* means three milks in Spanish. So that we don't hurt others with our words, we're going to practice counting to three: one means stop; two means think; and three means speak life.

COUNT TO TRES LECHES CAKE

Ingredients

1 cup all-purpose flour
1 ½ tsp. baking powder
¼ tsp. salt
5 large eggs
1 cup sugar (divide into ¾ cup and ¼ cup)
1 tsp. vanilla extract
⅓ cup whole milk (or oat milk for non-dairy)

Syrup

12 oz. evaporated milk
9 oz. sweetened condensed milk
⅓ cup heavy whipping cream
(*You can make this dairy-free with sweetened condensed coconut milk, evaporated coconut milk, and heavy coconut cream, or other non-dairy alternatives instead*)

Frosting

2 cups heavy whipping cream
2 tbsp. granulated sugar
1 cup fresh berries for garnishing, if desired

Directions

Preheat oven to 350°F and spray or butter a 13x9" cake pan.

In a large bowl, sift together flour, baking powder, and salt.

(You'll need two additional large bowls. If you have a stand mixer, I recommend putting the egg whites into that bowl and using an electric hand mixer for the yolks in the other bowl, or if you don't have a hand mixer, put the egg whites into a small bowl and do the yolk step in your stand mixer first, then wash the bowl before you mix the egg whites in your stand mixer as well.)

Separate the egg whites and yolks into two separate bowls.

Add ¾ cup sugar to the yolks and beat the mixture with an electric hand mixer on high for approximately two minutes, until they turn a pale yellow. Pour in the whole milk and vanilla extract and stir to combine.

In the bowl of your stand mixer with your whisk attachment (or with clean electric beaters), beat the egg whites on high speed until soft peaks form (approximately 1 minute). Keep the mixer on and add in ¼ cup sugar. Continue whipping on high until the egg whites form stiff peaks (approximately 1 more minute). *Stiff peaks* means when you pull the whisk out, the egg whites should keep their shape and not wilt like they did at soft peaks. *Don't overmix and allow them to become dry.*

Pour the egg yolk mixture over the flour mixture and use a spatula to combine.

Gently fold in the egg white mixture just until combined.

Pour the batter into your prepared pan and use the spatula to spread the mixture evenly in the pan.

Bake for 27-35 minutes, just until a toothpick inserted into the center of the cake comes out clean.

Clean your mixing bowl and place it in the refrigerator to chill for the whipped cream later.

While the cake is cooling, make the milk syrup.

In a large measuring cup, combine evaporated milk, sweetened condensed milk, and 1/3 cup heavy whipping cream. Stir to combine.

Once the cake has cooled, use a fork to poke holes all over (deep, but not clear through to the bottom of the cake).

Drizzle the milk mixture over the surface of the cake. (*It will look like you just ruined the cake with liquid, but you didn't, I promise! The liquid will be mostly absorbed by the cake.*)

For the frosting, use your chilled bowl and pour 2 cups heavy whipping cream and 2 tbsp. sugar into it. You can also add a teaspoon of vanilla extract if you'd like. Whip on high with whisk attachment for approximately two minutes, or until thick and spreadable.

Use a spatula to spread whipped cream frosting over the cake. *Best if chilled for at least an hour before serving, although overnight is even better.* Top with berries, if desired, before serving.

31

DISOBEDIENCE

Children, always obey your parents, for this pleases the Lord.
—Colossians 3:20

At times, parenting can feel like a battle as our kids argue about everything from chores to schoolwork to disagreements between siblings. I don't know about you, but sometimes, I'm just too tired to fight.

One day, my kids had failed to do something that I had requested of them. I couldn't tell you what exactly it was, but I clearly recall the moment I realized they had disobeyed. I was tired—tired of repeating myself and tired of correcting them. It wasn't a major thing, and it would have been so much easier to just take care of the matter myself in that moment, so that's exactly what I planned to do.

However, the Holy Spirit convicted me of the importance of addressing disobedience in my children's lives by reminding me of the prophet Samuel's words of warning to King Saul:

Rebellion is as sinful as witchcraft, and stubbornness as bad as worshiping idols. So because you have rejected the command of the LORD, he has rejected you as king. (1 Samuel 15:23)

In that moment, I realized just how critical it is that we teach our children to obey—not just us as parents, but all the authority God has placed in their lives. While a single act of disobedience may seem minor to us, it's a big deal to God—and we have no idea how many lives could be impacted by our actions.

I'm thankful that as young Christians, my husband and I participated in a church series on obedience and submitting to authority. It helped us navigate some of the most challenging battles we've faced in our faith walk. We learned to pray for our leaders, even when we disagree with them. We were taught to honor those in authority, not make fun of them or blast them on social media. And we learned how to navigate those times where someone in authority asks us to go against Scripture. These are the types of lessons we want to instill in our kids from a young age. They will carry our children far in life and in their walk with God.

Parents' Prayer

Holy Spirit, thank You for convicting me when I disobey. Forgive me for disobedience and help me to walk in the kind of faithful obedience that You desire as I teach my kids to do the same. In Jesus's name I pray. Amen.

Teachable Moment

In 1 Samuel 15, King Saul is sent to destroy the Amalekites. God specifically instructed him to kill every Amalekite and all of their animals. (See verse 3.) However, instead of doing it God's way, Saul decided to capture the king and keep the best of the animals. This single act of disobedience cost Saul his kingdom. When Saul tried to explain that he kept the animals and plunder to sacrifice to the Lord, Samuel had to explain the importance of obedience:

> But Samuel replied, "What is more pleasing to the LORD: your burnt offerings and sacrifices or your obedience to his voice? Listen! Obedience is better than sacrifice, and submission is better than offering the fat of rams." (1 Samuel 15:22)

God wants us to trust and obey Him in everything. Even when it's hard or doesn't make sense. Our obedience begins with obedience to God, but then extends outward to every other area of our lives. We are called to obey our parents, our spiritual leaders, and those in any position of authority in our lives, including our government leaders and appointed officials. The Bible teaches us that everyone in a position of authority has been placed there by God. (See Romans 13:1–7.)

Teach young kids to obey "all the way, right away, and with a good attitude." Emphasize the importance of doing what they are told instead of just what they want. It's helpful for children to understand clearly what's expected of them and the consequences for disobedience. If you don't have something in place already, now is a great time to write out a list of family rules and consequences as a family. This can help to eliminate disobedience because you're able to reference the family rules that you all agreed upon. I recommend typing this out as a living document so it can grow and change with your family.

For older kids or additional study, I've provided other Scriptures to help you dive deeper into the concept of obedience. Also, if your kids are older and you want to explore the topic of appropriate civil disobedience—when an authority figure asks you to violate God's commands—you can study some of these well-known biblical stories:

> » Hebrew midwives disobeyed Pharaoh when they were told to kill all the male Hebrew babies. (See Exodus 1:15–17.) Thus, Moses was spared and ended up leading his people out of Egypt.

> » Shadrach, Meshach, and Abednego refused to worship the statue of Nebuchadnezzar and ended up in the fiery furnace. (See Daniel 3.)

> » Daniel refused to worship the king and wound up in a lions' den. (See Daniel 6.)

» Paul was imprisoned repeatedly for preaching the gospel, which violated Roman law. (See, for example, Acts 16:20–24.)

Additional Scriptures for Study

On obeying our parents: "*Children, obey your parents because you belong to the Lord, for this is the right thing to do. 'Honor your father and mother.' This is the first commandment with a promise. If you honor your father and mother, 'things will go well for you, and you will have a long life on the earth'*" (Ephesians 6:1–3).

On obeying our spiritual leaders: "*Obey your spiritual leaders, and do what they say. Their work is to watch over your souls, and they are accountable to God. Give them reason to do this with joy and not with sorrow. That would certainly not be for your benefit*" (Hebrews 13:17).

On obeying government officials: "*Remind the believers to submit to the government and its officers. They should be obedient, always ready to do what is good. They must not slander anyone and must avoid quarreling. Instead, they should be gentle and show true humility to everyone*" (Titus 3:1–2). You can keep reading through verse 11 if you want to address how the Bible teaches us not to engage in useless arguments that stir up division.

For additional study, look up these Scriptures related to obedience and write them out: Joshua 5:6; Jeremiah 7:23; John 14:23–26, 15:14; Romans 6:16; Philippians 2:5–11; 1 Peter 2:13–21; 1 John 3:18–24.

Conversation Connection

» Who does the Bible teach us we need to obey? Why?

» Can you think of a time when disobedience has hurt you or others in some way?

» Can you think of a time when you obeyed even when it was hard? What happened?

» Is there ever a time when it is acceptable to disobey authority? How can you know if it's okay or not?

Family Fun

As a family, play the game Jesus Says, a variation of the game Simon Says. Take turns being Jesus and give instructions. The participants should obey whenever you begin with, "Jesus says..." If you give an instruction without that phrase and they do it, they're out. Remind them that it's important to listen to and obey Jesus and the authorities He has placed in our lives, such as parents, teachers, and employers. If your children are older, you can dive into a discussion of how to hear God's voice and discern His will for you.

Baking Buddies

Throughout both the Old and New Testaments, the Bible makes it clear that obedience matters. Today, we are making Obedient Oatmeal Raisin Cookies to help us remember to obey God and the authorities He has placed in our lives.

OBEDIENT OATMEAL RAISIN COOKIES (GLUTEN-FREE)

Ingredients

1 cup (2 sticks) unsalted butter, softened
1 cup brown sugar, packed
¼ cup granulated sugar
2 large eggs
1 tbsp. pure vanilla extract
½ tbsp. molasses
1 ½ cups 1:1 gluten-free baking flour (or regular all-purpose flour)
1 tsp. baking soda
¼ tsp. baking powder
1 ½ tsp. ground cinnamon
½ tsp. salt
3 cups gluten-free old-fashioned whole rolled oats (not instant)
1 cup raisins

Directions

In a medium bowl, whisk together flour, baking soda, baking powder, cinnamon, and salt just until combined. Set aside.

In the bowl of a stand mixer with paddle attachment (or using a large bowl with a hand mixer), cream butter and sugars on medium 1-2 minutes until creamy.

Add eggs and mix on high until incorporated.

Pour in vanilla and molasses. Scrape down the sides of the bowl and mix on high until combined.

Add dry ingredients into stand mixer. Mix on low until incorporated.

Pour oats and raisins into bowl and mix on low speed.

Cover with plastic wrap and chill dough in refrigerator for 30-60 minutes.

Once chilled, preheat oven to 350°F. Line two large baking sheets with parchment paper or silicone baking mats.

Roll dough into balls (approximately 2 tbsp. of dough) and place 2" apart on the prepared baking sheets. (*I like to use a large cookie scoop because the dough is sticky.*)

Bake 10-13 minutes until lightly browned on the sides. Centers will be soft and slightly underbaked, but shouldn't be glossy. If you use a smaller cookie scoop, reduce bake time to 7-9 minutes.

Allow to cool on cookie sheet for 4-5 minutes, then transfer to wire rack to finish cooling.

32

CRUSHES

Guard your heart above all else,
for it determines the course of your life.
—Proverbs 4:23

I'll never forget the day my kids were first exposed to the idea of "crushes." They were at a homeschool group when some other kids mentioned people they were infatuated with. Suddenly, my innocent five-year-old son went from being friends with a girl to being told he "had a crush" on her... to talking of marrying her someday! (Fortunately, as you may have guessed, *that* didn't work out.)

Crushes may seem innocent enough, but they're a gateway into rushed relationships and lusting after people. When we engage our hearts in that way, we start down a path of no return. Our hearts and minds become consumed with the idea of connection and dating relationships instead of friendships. We begin to imagine building a life with that person without fully understanding the commitment or consequences.

As parents, we all have our own thoughts and convictions when it comes to dating rules for our children. For many, age sixteen seems to be the magic number where they'll allow their teens to date. For our family, we felt convicted that dating would not be beneficial for our kids until they are old enough to realistically plan for marriage; any earlier and they were liable to enter into a relationship that could harm them. We've already discussed this topic in depth with our kids, who are both under ten. We talk about keeping our hearts pure and protecting them from a young age.

I used to think that many challenging topics could be put off until our kids were older. However, I quickly realized that children are being exposed to a highly sexualized world at a young age. It's our job to provide truth and guidance so they aren't left to the whims of this wacky world.

In my years of experience as a counselor—and in youth, young adult, and marriage ministry—I've seen the impact of giving your heart away too freely and too early. These relationships are often cultivated for pleasure, which ultimately leads us astray. Our children need to learn how to intentionally pursue God and let the Holy Spirit lead and guide in relationships.

Parents' Prayer

Jesus, protect our children's innocence and guard their hearts and minds. Help them make wise decisions regarding relationships as they grow and give me the words to speak to help them navigate the challenges they'll face. In Jesus's name I pray. Amen.

Teachable Moment

Proverbs 4:23 warns us, *"Guard your heart above all else, for it determines the course of your life."* What do you think it means to guard your heart?

Throughout your life, you will encounter many wonderful people, but you must not give your heart away before marriage. For a visual, cut out a large construction paper heart and decorate it with your child's name. Explain that if they allow themselves to have a "crush" on someone, they give that person a piece of their heart (rip off a piece). Even if you only give a piece or two away before you're married, you won't have a complete heart to give your spouse when you meet them. Broken hearts can lead to broken marriages, so we should diligently protect our heart and save it for the right person. You can try to take the pieces of your heart back after you've given them away, but your heart will never be the same. Try to put the paper heart back together with tape or glue. Notice how this is cannot restore it to its original form.

The Bible teaches us that we *"are all children of God"* (Galatians 3:26), brothers and sisters in Christ. (See Matthew 12:48–50.) So when we meet someone we like or feel attracted to, we want to honor and treat them as a brother or sister in Christ. In addition to guarding our hearts, the Bible urges us to guard our thoughts too. Philippians 4:8 says, *"And now, dear brothers and sisters, one final thing. Fix your thoughts on what is true, and honorable, and right, and pure, and lovely, and admirable. Think about things that are excellent and worthy of praise."*

Conversation Connection

» Why is it important to guard your heart?

» What can happen if you give your heart away to the wrong person?

» How can you pray for a person you like? How should you think of them?

» What can you do when your friends start talking about having crushes?

Family Fun

We're going to play the Guard Your Heart Game, a variation of Capture the Flag. Get two pieces of construction paper of different colors or two pieces of cloth and cut them out into heart shapes. You can connect them to a stick or straw or leave them as is. Divide into two teams. Create a base for each team where the heart is placed. The goal is to try to capture the other team's heart and return it to your base while protecting your heart from them. The team that first captures and returns the other team's heart to their base wins. If you are tagged by the other team while trying to capture their flag, you're stuck in place until someone from your team comes and tags you to rescue you. Remind your family that we always want to guard and protect our hearts. If you don't have enough players or space for this game, you can hide the hearts somewhere in the house and race to find the other player's heart first. You can encourage your kids to hide their hearts and seek the Lord.

Baking Buddies

Proverbs 4:23 says, "*Guard your heart above all else, for it determines the course of your life.*" Today we're making Guard Your Heart Raspberry Rolls to remind us to protect our hearts and keep them pure.

GUARD YOUR HEART
RASPBERRY ROLLS

Ingredients

Dough

1 cup lukewarm whole milk
1/3 cup lukewarm water
1 pkg. instant yeast
3 tbsp. granulated sugar
3 ½ cups all-purpose flour
1 tsp. salt

Filling

10 oz. frozen raspberries
⅓ cup granulated sugar
1 tsp. cornstarch
1 tsp. orange zest (zest the top of the peel from 1 orange)

Sugar Icing

1 cup powdered sugar
1-2 tbsp. milk
1 tsp. pure vanilla extract

OR Cream Cheese Icing

8 oz. cream cheese (softened to room temperature)
1 ¼ cup powdered sugar
⅓ cup heavy whipping cream

Directions

Preheat oven to 350°F. Grease two 9" pie pans or 9x13" baking pan.

Warm milk in microwave-safe measuring cup for 15-30 seconds. It should be warm but not hot.

In the bowl of your stand mixer with the dough hook, combine all of the dough ingredients on speed 2 and knead for 5 minutes (or until dough is smooth).

Use a handful of flour to spread onto your counter or work surface and turn the dough out of the bowl onto the floured surface. Cover with a towel or plastic wrap and allow the dough to rest for 10 minutes.

In a medium bowl, combine the frozen raspberries, cornstarch, sugar, and orange zest. Stir to combine.

Coat your rolling pin in flour, then roll out your rested dough into a rectangle approximately 9x15".

Spread the raspberry mixture evenly over the surface of the dough.

Start on the long edge of the rectangle and roll the dough tightly toward the center. Stop at the center of the dough.

From the other long edge, roll the dough tightly toward the center until both sides meet in the middle. Gently press the sides together to form the top of the hearts.

Parents, use a sharp knife to cut off the ends (for clean lines), then slice the dough into 10 equal pieces.

To make the heart shapes, pinch the bottoms of each piece with your fingers to form the bottom point of the heart and press the top centers together better if needed. Place the pieces in your prepared pan with the pointed ends in the center of the pan (five per pie pan).

Bake for 20-25 minutes, until they are lightly golden brown.

Allow them to cool in the pan for several minutes before transferring to a wire rack to finish cooling.

If making the vanilla icing, in a small bowl, combine powdered sugar and vanilla with 1 tbsp. milk. Whisk together and add additional tbsp. of milk to reach desired consistency (thick but able to drizzle).

If making the cream cheese icing, use an electric hand mixer to beat the cream cheese for 1-2 minutes, then add in the powdered sugar a bit at a time until incorporated. Pour in the heavy cream and beat for several more minutes until fluffy.

Place icing in a small plastic bag and seal. Cut a tiny hole in the bottom corner and use as a piping bag to drizzle over the rolls before serving.

33

FAIRNESS

The workers who were hired at five o'clock came to get their pay.
Each worker got one silver coin. Then the workers who were hired first
came to get their pay. They thought they would be paid more than the
others. But each one of them also received one silver coin.
When they got their silver coin, they complained to the man who
owned the land. They said, "Those people were hired last and worked
only one hour. But you paid them the same as us. And we worked
hard all day in the hot sun." But the man who owned the field said to
one of them, "Friend, I am being fair with you. You agreed to work
for one silver coin. Right? So take your pay and go. I want to give the
man who was hired last the same pay I gave you. I can do what I
want with my own money. Why would you be jealous because I am
generous?" So those who are last now will be first in the future.
And those who are first now will be last in the future.
—Matthew 20:9–16 (ERV)

This concept of fairness is embedded within us from birth. We hear our toddlers whining, "That's not fair" when we've never even said the word *fair* to them. I'm still trying to figure that one out. But I've found that it's especially bad when you put two kids together. Suddenly, their favorite phrase becomes, "That's not fair!" And of course, being the stellar parent we all know that I am, my oh so elegant response tends to be, "Well, life's not fair."

But when we really examine the idea of fairness, it gets even more convoluted. Fair to whom? What seems fair to my nine-year-old daughter seems unfair to my six-year-old son. And vice versa. Not to mention what seems fair to me or my husband in the same situation. How about fairness to our neighbors or to God?

The truth is that fairness is a relative concept that by its very nature is unfair. It isn't fair that God sent His only Son to die for our sins so we could live eternally with Him. It isn't fair that God has blessed us and done the miraculous for us, yet we repeatedly sin against Him and disobey Him. It isn't fair that we often don't appreciate what He has given us or how He makes all things work together for our good. Yet by God's grace and mercy, we get to live this unfair life with the hope of an eternity we don't deserve.

We aren't bound and limited by the world's system of fairness because God's unmerited favor isn't fair. It wasn't fair that young Joseph was esteemed above all his siblings, or that the shepherd boy David was anointed king instead of one of his older brothers. It certainly wasn't fair that Saul, the man who killed and persecuted Christians, became the great apostle Paul who wrote approximately two-thirds of the New Testament.

The sooner we can free our children from the constraints and trappings of the concept of fairness, the better off they'll be. Only then can they break free from a victim mindset and live their lives as powerful sons and daughters of God who passionately pursue their callings and serve others instead of seeking gain for themselves.

Parents' Prayer

Father God, forgive me for times I've fallen into this trap of fairness. Thank You for Your grace and mercy. Help me to lead my children to live a life worthy of Your calling and to love others as You have loved us. In Jesus's name I pray. Amen.

Teachable Moment

If you have more than one child, explain to them that you have decided to give the punishment for everyone's sins or bad choices to one of your children. (If you have an only child, you can tell them you intend to give them the punishment for all their friends' sins or your sins. For really young kids, you may need to explain that they're going to get in trouble every time anyone does anything bad or wrong.) Ask how they'd feel about that. Does that seem fair? Jesus never did anything wrong in His entire life. He was blameless. Yet He took the punishment for everything bad committed by every single person who ever lived and everyone yet to be born, just so we could spend eternity with Him. Does that seem fair?

For everyone has sinned; we all fall short of God's glorious standard. Yet God, in his grace, freely makes us right in his sight. He did this through Christ Jesus when he freed us from the penalty for our sins. For God presented Jesus as the sacrifice for sin. People are made right with God when they believe that Jesus sacrificed his life, shedding his blood. This sacrifice shows that God was being fair when he held back and did not punish those who sinned in times past, for he was looking ahead and including them in what he would do in this present time. God did this to demonstrate his righteousness, for he himself is fair and just, and he makes sinners right in his sight when they believe in Jesus.

(Romans 3:23–26)

You could also recreate the parable of the vineyard workers in Matthew 20:1–16 with your kids. Explain that you are going to pay your child a certain amount to do some hard task that they would gladly do in order to earn money. (Choose the child who struggles with fairness the most.) Have them get started. Depending on how many kids you have, send them in one at a time to help with the task, until you send one in right before the task is finished. Have them all line up along the wall for their payment. Start with one who came in last and give them the wage that you promised to the first. Say aloud, "Here's your dollar for cleaning the baseboards," or cleaning the garage, raking leaves, or some other chore that's time-consuming. Then continue on until you get to the first child and offer the same amount you promised. See how they respond. If they struggle, explain that the vineyard workers in the Bible wrestled with this same issue. If they don't complain, praise them for their reasonableness and share the story from Matthew 20.

Discuss why the workers felt they were treated unfairly, why they think the owner was so generous, and how we can apply the lesson to our own lives.

Conversation Connection

»   What is the most unfair thing in the entire world? (*Jesus receiving the punishment for all our sins*). How can that knowledge help us when we're wrestling with something that doesn't seem fair?

»   Why do you think we all struggle with the idea of fairness?

»   How can worrying about things being fair create problems for us? (*Jealousy, bitterness, unforgiveness, hatred, disobedience, rebellion, ungratefulness, etc.*)

»   What can you do the next time you're feeling upset that something doesn't seem fair?

Family Fun

As a family, create your own It's *Not* a Competition Olympic Games. Choose one game, event, or activity for each member of the family. Think of the unique strengths or giftings of each person. What would Dad be better at than anyone else? Mom? Each kid? Ask if they have any predictions or guesses about who might be the best at each event. Explain that at the Olympic Games, the best doesn't always win. Why might that be? King Solomon, the wisest man who ever lived, tells us this:

I also saw other things in this life that were not fair. The fastest runner does not always win the race; the strongest soldier does not always win the battle; wise people don't always get the food; smart people don't always get the wealth; educated people don't always get the praise they deserve. When the time comes, bad things can happen to anyone! You never know when hard times will come. Like fish in a net or birds in a snare, people are often trapped by some disaster that suddenly falls on them. (Ecclesiastes 9:11–12 ERV)

Have fun doing each event together. Explain that God has made each of us unique. There are no two people who have ever lived—or who will ever exist in the future—who are exactly the same. We can't compare our lives to anyone else, which means we need to break free from the lie that things need to be *fair*, and instead focus on our own lives and purposes.

Pay careful attention to your own work, for then you will get the satisfaction of a job well done, and you won't need to compare yourself to anyone else. For we are each responsible for our own conduct. (Galatians 6:4–5)

Baking Buddies

God created each person uniquely. We know this because we all have different DNA and fingerprints. Today we're making Fingerprint of God Peanut Butter Kiss Cookies to remind us that God's thumbprint is on each of us, so we don't need to worry about what seems fair, only doing what is right in every situation. The kiss on top reminds us of God's great love for us, even when the world seems unfair.

FINGERPRINT OF GOD PEANUT BUTTER KISS COOKIES

Ingredients

1 ¾ cups all-purpose flour
1 tsp. baking soda
½ tsp. salt
½ cup (1 stick) butter, softened to room temperature
½ cup creamy peanut butter (or other smooth nut butter)
½ cup granulated sugar (plus more to roll cookies in)
½ cup light brown sugar
1 large egg
1 tbsp. half-and-half or milk
1 tsp. vanilla extract
1 pkg. Hershey's Kisses (unwrapped)

Directions

Unwrap about 24 candy kisses and set aside.

In a medium bowl, sift together flour, baking soda, and salt. Set aside.

In the bowl of your stand mixer (or another large bowl with an electric hand mixer), cream together butter, peanut butter, brown sugar, and ½ cup granulated sugar until light and creamy.

Add in milk, egg, and vanilla, beating until well-blended.

Gradually pour in flour mixture and mix until fully incorporated.

Cover bowl with plastic wrap and chill dough for 30-60 minutes in the refrigerator.

Preheat oven to 375°F and line a couple cookie sheets with parchment paper.

Use a small cookie scoop or your hands to make balls approximately 1" each.

Place extra sugar in a small bowl (about ½ cup) and roll the balls of dough in the sugar before placing them on the prepared baking sheets (2" apart).

Gently press your thumb into the center of each cookie to form a slight indentation.

Place tray with cookies into the refrigerator for 10 minutes to chill (it helps them keep their shape better).

Bake 6-7 minutes until they turn a light brown color.

An adult should remove sheet from oven and carefully place an unwrapped candy kiss in the center of each cookie.

Put cookies back into the oven for an additional 2-3 minutes.

Allow them to cool on cookie sheet for a couple minutes before removing to a wire rack with a spatula to finish cooling.

If you wish, while waiting for cookies to bake, place a small amount of flour into a bowl. Grab a piece of darkly colored paper, some tape, and a pen or pencil. Let everyone dip their thumb into the flour, then put a small piece of tape over their thumb to capture their thumbprint. Carefully remove the tape and place it on the paper. Label everyone's thumbprint and examine the unique design of each print, using a magnifying glass if you have one. Talk about how amazing our God is and how He has created each of us uniquely.

34

CLIQUES/EXCLUDING OTHERS

I appeal to you, dear brothers and sisters,
by the authority of our Lord Jesus Christ, to live in harmony with
each other. Let there be no divisions in the church.
Rather, be of one mind, united in thought and purpose.
—1 Corinthians 1:10

Have you ever been left out? I certainly have. Relationships can be tricky, even for adults. Our kids need guidance to navigate the intricacies of interpersonal communication and conduct in order to cultivate healthy relationships throughout their lives.

Maybe your child is feeling left out, or perhaps your child is the one leaving someone else out. Regardless of which side of the coin they're on, there are many things we can do to help them build strong, beneficial relationships.

We all have different personalities, strengths, and challenges when it comes to our dealings with others. As our children grow, we get a better understanding of who they are and how we can best support them. But until that picture begins to form, we can always start with the basics of relationship-building—things like kindness, compassion, communication, boundaries, social awareness, and empathy.

And as our kids grow, we can teach them skills more tailored to their unique situations. For me personally, I had to learn how to be more outgoing, how to set healthy boundaries, and how to spend time by myself to recharge. I'm an extroverted introvert surrounded by extroverted extroverts who can't seem to get enough of people...while I'm happy to just be by myself.

Our daughter has needed support in approaching others, working through conflict, and being okay by herself when others exclude her. She prefers deep relationships with one or two people. Our son, on the other hand, is like a magnet, and the more people playing together, the happier he seems to be. When he meets new people, they quickly become friends. At times, however, he struggles to set boundaries and clearly communicate his needs.

How about your kids? What are their relational strengths and challenges?

As Christians, we're called to unity, to love our neighbors as ourselves. Healthy relationships matter. God uses relationships to mold and refine us. They're essential in building the kingdom of God, and it requires intentionality if we're going to equip our kids to thrive.

Parents' Prayer

Jesus, forgive me for times where I've excluded others. Heal any wounds created within me when others have excluded me. Show me how to disciple my kids to build healthy relationships and be a good friend to all. In Jesus's name I pray. Amen.

Teachable Moment

God has called us to be gatherers, not excluders. He wants us to live in unity as the body of Christ, realizing that each of us has a unique value and purpose. Ephesians 4:1–4 says:

Therefore I, a prisoner for serving the Lord, beg you to lead a life worthy of your calling, for you have been called by God. Always be humble and gentle. Be patient with each other, making allowance for each other's faults because of your love. Make every effort to keep yourselves united in Spirit, binding yourselves together with peace. For there is one body and one Spirit, just as you have been called to one glorious hope for the future.

For older kids, write out these verses and have them highlight the most important words in the passage. Discuss what each sentence means and how they can apply it to their lives right now. For younger kids, you could cut one-inch strips of different colored paper and glue the ends together to make a paper chain. Give each person a few strips for their chain. Decorate them if you wish. You could even write out all of their gifts, talents, and positive qualities on each chain. Then explain how much better we are when we band together, enabling us to go further and do more. When we exclude someone, we break the chain. Link all of the chains together and display them somewhere in the house.

For another activity, a Mr. Potato Head toy makes an excellent visual. You can also use a book on human anatomy, a puzzle, or simply have a discussion. Ask your kids to think about the body and which parts they consider most important. What parts do they think they could live without? Explain that we are our best when we live in harmony with other people, just like our body works best with all of its many parts. God has created us to need other people. We are most effective together. Every person has something unique to offer. Read 1 Corinthians 12:12–14, 18–27:

The human body has many parts, but the many parts make up one whole body. So it is with the body of Christ. Some of us are Jews, some are Gentiles, some are slaves, and some are free. But we have all been baptized into one body by one Spirit, and we all share the same Spirit. Yes, the body has many different parts, not just one part…God has put each part just where he wants it. How strange a body would be if it had only one part! Yes, there are many parts, but only one body. The eye can never say to the hand, "I don't need you." The head can't say to the feet, "I don't need you." In fact, some parts of the body that seem weakest and least important are actually the most necessary. And the parts we regard as less honorable are those we clothe with the greatest care. So we carefully protect those parts that should not be seen, while the more honorable parts do not require this special care. So God has put the body together such that extra honor and care are given to those parts that have less dignity. This makes for harmony among the members, so that all the members care for each other. If one part suffers, all the parts suffer with it, and if one part is honored, all the parts are glad. All of you together are Christ's body, and each of you is a part of it.

Jesus was known for loving even the most unlovable people, and He asks us to share that same love with everyone we meet. We can't change how other people act, but we can choose how *we* will act.

If Your Child Has Been Excluding Others

Talk about ways that they can include others and discuss the importance of asking for forgiveness when we've wronged someone else. Read Colossians 3:12–14 and discuss what it means and how they can apply it to this situation:

Since God chose you to be the holy people he loves, you must clothe yourselves with tenderhearted mercy, kindness, humility, gentleness, and patience. Make allowance for each other's faults, and forgive anyone who offends you. Remember, the Lord forgave you, so you must forgive others. Above all, clothe yourselves with love, which binds us all together in perfect harmony.

If Your Child Has Been Excluded by Others

Talk about the power of forgiving those who've hurt us—even if they keep doing it and never apologize. Explain that Jesus tells us to forgive because God has forgiven us. Remind them that someone leaving them out is really about their own hurts and issues, not your child's. Brainstorm ways your child can include other people and love like Jesus. Luke 6:27–31 says:

> But to you who are willing to listen, I say, love your enemies! Do good to those who hate you. Bless those who curse you. Pray for those who hurt you. If someone slaps you on one cheek, offer the other cheek also. If someone demands your coat, offer your shirt also. Give to anyone who asks; and when things are taken away from you, don't try to get them back. Do to others as you would like them to do to you.

Conversation Connection

» Have you ever been excluded? How did it feel? What did you do?

» What can you do if you see someone by themselves?

» Do you think Jesus ever felt excluded? What did He do?

» Why does the Bible say we are better together?

» How can we become known as gatherers instead of excluders?

Family Fun

We're going to play Better Together Balloon War. Blow up three balloons per person. Spread out and instruct everyone that when you say, "Go!" each person must attempt to keep all three balloons in the air by themselves, using any part of their body—but they can't hold the balloons or let them rest anywhere on their bodies. As soon as one balloon touches the ground, they're out. Try this one or two times. Then, work together to keep three balloons up in the air and see how long you can do it when you work together. Afterward, explain, "We're on a battlefield of life, but we aren't meant to fight alone." Ecclesiastes 4:9–12 says:

Two people are better off than one, for they can help each other succeed.
If one person falls, the other can reach out and help. But someone who
falls alone is in real trouble. Likewise, two people lying close together
can keep each other warm. But how can one be warm alone? A person
standing alone can be attacked and defeated, but two can stand back-
to-back and conquer. Three are even better, for a triple-braided cord is
not easily broken.

Each person has something wonderful inside of them to offer the world. We only discover those gifts when we include everyone.

If your child has struggled with excluding others, you could ask them to stand on the sidelines and watch while the rest of the family played. Then discuss how it feels to be excluded from the fun. Explain that we always want to find ways to include others.

If your child has been hurt by others excluding them, explain that even if others exclude us, we can choose to love and lead like Jesus by seeking to always include others and reach out to people who have been excluded. Remind them that Jesus says, *"If the world hates you, remember that it hated me first. The world would love you as one of its own if you belonged to it, but you are no longer part of the world. I chose you to come out of the world, so it hates you"* (John 15:18–19). You may feel hated by the world, but always remember that you are loved and chosen by God. Someone choosing to exclude you says everything about them and nothing about you.

Baking Buddies

The Bible talks about Jesus as our bridegroom and us, His church, as His bride.

"Let us be glad and rejoice, and let us give honor to him. For the time
has come for the wedding feast of the Lamb, and his bride has prepared
herself. She has been given the finest of pure white linen to wear." For
the fine linen represents the good deeds of God's holy people.

(Revelation 19:7–8)

We want to invite everyone we can to the wedding feast so they can live eternally with Christ in heaven. Today we're making Bride of Christ Brown Butter Wedding Cookies to help us remember to include everyone so they can meet Jesus through our love and good deeds.

BRIDE OF CHRIST BROWN BUTTER WEDDING COOKIES

Ingredients

- 1 cup (2 sticks) unsalted butter
- 1 cup pecans or walnuts (optional)
- ½ tsp. kosher salt
- 1 ½ cups powdered sugar, divided
- 2 cups all-purpose flour
- 1 tsp. pure vanilla extract
- ¼ cup milk

Directions

In a small skillet over medium heat, melt the butter. (*Caution: butter will be extremely hot and will pop a bit, so an adult should do this step.*) Stir continually with a rubber spatula for 6-8 minutes. The butter will foam and smell nutty, creating little golden-brown pieces at the bottom. Once that happens, carefully pour the butter into a medium heatproof bowl and leave in the refrigerator for 30-60 minutes so that it starts to solidify.

Finely chop the walnuts or pecans (you can also use an alternative nut or leave them out if allergic) or quickly pulse in a food processor.

Add salt and ½ cup of powdered sugar to the chilled butter and beat on high with an electric mixer for approximately three minutes, until light and fluffy.

Add flour to mixture and beat until combined, using a rubber spatula to scrape the sides of bowl as needed.

Pour vanilla and milk into batter and stir to incorporate. Then fold in the nuts.

Cover bowl with plastic wrap and chill in refrigerator for approximately an hour until the dough firms up.

Once the dough has chilled, preheat oven to 325°F and line a baking sheet with parchment paper (or spray with nonstick spray if you don't have parchment paper).

Use a small cookie scoop or your hands to make 1" balls and place them approximately 2" apart on the prepared cookie sheet. I recommend placing them back in the fridge or freezer for an additional 10 minutes so they keep their shape better.

Sift the remaining cup of powdered sugar into a large bowl.

Bake the cookies for 10 minutes, then rotate the pan 180°F and bake for an additional 10-12 minutes. You want them to start to look dry but not turn brown.

Allow the cookies to cool on the cookie sheet for several minutes so they are cool enough to handle but still warm. Gently toss them in the powdered sugar and then transfer to a wire rack to finish cooling.

Once the cookies have cooled completely, toss a second time in the powdered sugar. Store in an airtight container at room temperature overnight and enjoy immediately or store in an airtight container for the next day.

35

REJECTION

If the world hates you, remember that it hated me first.
The world would love you as one of its own if you belonged to it,
but you are no longer part of the world.
I chose you to come out of the world, so it hates you.
—John 15:18–19

Nothing stings quite like rejection. Whether it's not being picked for a team, chosen for an award, or selected for a job, no one likes to feel rejected. I used to wrestle with rejection, wondering why people hated me who didn't even know me or didn't know me well. I wondered what was wrong with *me* and spent a good chunk of my life feeling inadequate.

However, Jesus changed all of that. The closer I drew to Jesus, the more I realized that it wasn't *me* being rejected—it was Him. The Bible teaches us that our battle is not with people. We see this in Ephesians 6:10–12:

A final word: Be strong in the Lord and in his mighty power. Put on all of God's armor so that you will be able to stand firm against all the strategies of the devil. For we are not fighting against flesh-and-blood enemies, but against evil rulers and authorities of the unseen world, against mighty powers in this dark world, and against evil spirits in the heavenly places.

Our young daughter shines brightly for Jesus, but she has experienced an incredible amount of rejection over the past few years. As painful as these experiences have been for both Kendra and me, they've also created opportunities to share powerful truths over her that will carry her throughout the trials of this life.

The truth is, we are not of this world, and this is not our home. God has created us to be set apart. Because we are marked by God, we will inevitably be rejected by people. As long as we keep our eyes fixed on Jesus, standing on His promises, we will persevere and receive the crown of life. We have been chosen by God, and that is a priceless gift.

Helping our kids change their perspective when they experience rejection builds up their spiritual muscles and gives them invaluable life skills. We will all face rejection, but how we respond to it can determine the trajectory of our lives. Will we give up when things get hard or don't go our way? Will we become bitter and offended? Or will we persevere and grow through the difficulties? Remember, rejection can also be God's redirection.

Parents' Prayer

Heavenly Father, comfort me and my children when we experience rejection. Help us to stand firm on Your truth and Your promises. Guard our hearts and our minds and grant us wisdom in those difficult situations. In Jesus's name I pray. Amen.

Teachable Moment

Jesus was rejected many times—rejected by His family (see John 7:5–7), his hometown of Nazareth (Matthew 13:53–58), and the religious leaders (see, for example, Matthew 12:14). In fact, the world chose to save the life of a murderer and crucify Jesus even though He hadn't done anything wrong. (Read Luke 23:1–25...or continue on to read through the crucifixion as well.)

You could turn back to Luke 22:31–65 and talk about how Jesus's close friend and disciple Judas betrayed Jesus and then Peter rejected Him before the guards mocked and insulted Him. Write about the thoughts and feelings that occur when we experience rejection. (*I'm not loved, I'm not valuable, there's something wrong with me, I'm not good enough, etc.*)

Explain that when people reject us, they are often really rejecting God.

Then he said to the disciples, "Anyone who accepts your message is also accepting me. And anyone who rejects you is rejecting me. And anyone who rejects me is rejecting God, who sent me." (Luke 10:16)

For younger kids, share one or two verses about being loved, accepted, and chosen by God and help them memorize these. (For example, Ephesians 1:4–5; 1 Thessalonians 1:4; Isaiah 54:10.) For older kids, I encourage you to help them find verses to refute each of the negative thoughts they struggle with when experiencing rejection. Write out the thought in one column and the truth from God's Word in the second column.

See how very much our Father loves us, for he calls us his children, and that is what we are! But the people who belong to this world don't recognize that we are God's children because they don't know him. (1 John 3:1)

For additional activities, you can research or share about famous people in history who experienced rejection, but persevered and didn't give up. For example, Michael Jordan was cut from his high school basketball team, Walt Disney was fired from a newspaper and told he didn't have any good ideas, and Henry Ford's first and second automobile companies went bankrupt.

Conversation Connection

» Why do you think rejection hurts so bad?

» What can you tell yourself the next time you're rejected?

» How did Jesus respond to rejection? What can we learn from Him?

» Think of a recent rejection. How might that situation be redirecting you?

Family Fun

Today we're going to play the Rejection Protection Game so we can practice how to respond to rejection. Write out a list of experiences in which someone might face rejection, such as interviewing for a job and not being hired, entering a contest and not winning, trying out for a team and not being selected, applying for college and not being admitted, asking to play with other kids and being told "no," or inviting someone to church and having them turn you down. Take turns picking one scenario and acting it out. Discuss how to respond and what you can do next. Remember, Peter wrote:

> *Friends, this world is not your home, so don't make yourselves cozy in it. Don't indulge your ego at the expense of your soul. Live an exemplary life in your neighborhood so that your actions will refute their prejudices. Then they'll be won over to God's side and be there to join in the celebration when he arrives.* (1 Peter 2:11–12 MSG)

Baking Buddies

Although people may reject us, God never will. Psalm 94:14 assures us, "The LORD will not reject his people; he will not abandon his special possession."

Today, we're making God's Golden Possessions Turmeric Muffins to remind us that we are being refined like gold when we persevere through hurts and rejections. God promises that He will not reject or abandon us, for we are His special possessions.

GOD'S GOLDEN POSSESSIONS
TURMERIC MUFFINS (GLUTEN-FREE)

Ingredients

1/3 cup melted coconut oil

2 large eggs

⅔ cup unsweetened applesauce

⅓ cup pure maple syrup

1 tsp. pure vanilla extract

2 ⅓ almond flour (can also use regular all-purpose flour or oat flour instead)

½ tsp. baking soda

½ tsp. baking powder

¼ tsp. kosher salt

2 tsp. ground turmeric

½ tsp. ground cinnamon

½ tsp. ground ginger

⅛ tsp. fresh ground pepper (*yes*—black pepper to help activate the turmeric)

⅔ cup chocolate chips, (reserve 1/3 cup for sprinkling on top)

Directions

Preheat oven to 350°F and either line 12 muffin tins with paper liners or grease them so they don't stick.

In a large bowl, combine oil, eggs, syrup, applesauce, and vanilla. Whisk to combine.

Pour in the flour, baking soda, baking powder, salt, turmeric, black pepper, cinnamon, and ginger. Stir until fully incorporated.

Add in 1/3 cup of the chocolate chips and stir to combine.

Use a large cookie scoop or small measuring cup to scoop the batter into your prepared muffin tins. Fill each cup 2/3 full (approximately ¼ cup of batter).

Top each muffin with more chocolate chips and press them gently into the top of the batter.

Bake for 15-20 minutes, or until a toothpick inserted into the center comes out clean (you'll notice the muffins pulling away from the sides of the pan).

Let the muffins cool in the pan for about five minutes before removing to a wire rack to finish cooling.

36

FOLLOWING THE CROWD

You can enter God's Kingdom only through the narrow gate. T
he highway to hell is broad, and its gate is wide for the many who
choose that way. But the gateway to life is very narrow and
the road is difficult, and only a few ever find it.
—Matthew 7:13–14

Perhaps some of the most challenging experiences we faced by following the crowd came when we signed up for a Christian homeschool group in a city we had just moved to. It turned out that all of the families had a deep obsession with a popular phenomenon that our kids knew they weren't allowed to watch, or play with or own its representative toys. Unfortunately, that's what all of the other children talked about, wore on their clothing, brought to play with before and after the group sessions, and shared about during presentation time. *Every. Single. Week.* Despite my kids' best efforts to offer playtime alternatives, they were often left out or stuck participating in made-up games related to this pop culture thing. I was committed to a contract to help out for the school year, so we couldn't just quit or change groups.

It was a difficult year for all of us, but an especially trying one for our daughter. Kendra has a strong sense of right and wrong, as well as a sensitive spirit, so participating in a group in which she was surrounded by what she knew went against our values and beliefs created many challenges for her. She struggled to know how to interact and guard herself when she couldn't escape what went against her convictions or simply remove herself fully from the situation.

Yet, through all the challenges, we didn't stand on a platform to tell those families why they shouldn't watch those shows, play those games, or do those things. I didn't engage in heated debates about why the pop pastime was evil or stir up strife. Our family simply did our best to love them and honor God with our words and actions while we were among them. Peter writes:

> *It is God's will that your honorable lives silence those ignorant people who make foolish accusations against you. For you are free, yet you are God's slaves, so don't use your freedom as an excuse to do evil. Respect everyone, and love the family of believers. Fear God, and respect the king.* (1 Peter 2:15–17)

I wish I could say this year was an isolated event, but this type of struggle has become more of the norm than the exception for us. We've committed our lives to following Jesus at any cost. And while many call themselves Christians, few actually make Jesus Lord of their lives. We've found that even among church leadership, we stand out because we refuse to compromise in many of the ways other Christians have.

Around the world, many believers have compromised their faith, living either as complacent Christians paralyzed by fear of cancel culture or as clanging gongs beating other people over the head with their own self-righteousness. I believe we must lead with love while not being ashamed to stand out. We can't change the world if we're following the crowd instead of Jesus.

Parents' Prayer

Father God, forgive me for areas where I've compromised or treated others poorly. Give me the strength to lead with love and guide my children along Your path instead of following the crowd. In Jesus's name I pray. Amen.

Teachable Moment

Have you ever tried to go against the crowd? Like walking up the stairs when everyone else is going down? It's not easy, and it doesn't often feel good in the moment, but when you reach your destination, the reward will be worth the struggle. If you have stairs, you can try to (carefully) demonstrate this, or you can mark a line on the floor and have everyone but one person link arms. The person who is not part of the crowd attempts to break through the crowd and cross the finish line, while the crowd keeps themselves together and tries to stop them from reaching their goal.

» It can be hard not to follow the crowd, but the Bible warns us in Proverbs 14:12–13 (MSG), "*There's a way of life that looks harmless enough; look again—it leads straight to hell. Sure, those people appear to be having a good time, but all that laughter will end in heartbreak.*" Talk about situations in which your children are struggling because they want to follow the crowd and discuss how or why those behaviors are harmful.

» Isaiah 8:11–13 (ERV) says, "*The LORD spoke to me with his great power and warned me not to be like these people. He said, 'Don't think there is a plan against you just because the people say there is. Don't be afraid of what they fear. Don't let them frighten you!' The LORD All-Powerful is the one you should fear. He is the one you should respect. He is the one who should frighten you.*" (To fear the Lord doesn't mean to be afraid of Him, but to honor, respect, and be in awe of Him. He is the Creator of all things, all-powerful, all-knowing, and worthy of all praise.) How does the fear of the Lord help us overcome the fear of man and desire to follow the crowd?

» Romans 12:2 (ERV) tells us, "*Don't change yourselves to be like the people of this world, but let God change you inside with a new way of thinking. Then you will be able to understand and accept what God wants for you. You will be able to know what is good and pleasing to him and what is perfect.*" What is one way you have tried to change yourself to be accepted by others? How can you let God change the way you think instead?

Conversation Connection

» Can you think of a time when you followed the crowd, even though you knew you shouldn't? What happened? What could you have done differently?

» Why do you think it's easier to follow the crowd than to go against it?

» How do we know if something is right or wrong? (*Just because everyone's doing it doesn't make it right, and just because no one else is doing it doesn't make it wrong.*)

» What can you do to help make it easier to follow Jesus instead of the crowd?

Family Fun

It's time to play Whose Voice Should You Follow? Blindfold one person and place them at one end of the room. Spin them around a few times. Have everyone else stand across the room and explain that the goal is to follow their father's or mother's voice and try to tag them. But everyone else is to shout and encourage the person to come to them instead. They win if they get to the right person and lose if they follow the wrong voice. For older kids, you can make an obstacle course with things that could trip them up, such as a kiddie pool with water, and try to lead them through the course with your voice while others try to lead them astray. Jesus tells us, "*My sheep listen to my voice; I know them, and they follow me*" (John 10:27). The world is loud in its attempts to lead us down the wrong path, which is why we must learn to listen to Jesus's voice instead and allow Him to lead us along the best path for our lives. The more time we spend with Him by praying, reading the Bible, and worshipping Him, the easier it becomes to hear and obey His voice.

Baking Buddies

Proverbs 13:20 says, "*Walk with the wise and become wise; associate with fools and get in trouble.*" When we follow Jesus instead of the crowd, the world calls us wacky, but God calls us wise. Noah seemed wacky to his neighbors as he built the ark—until the flood came. He followed God instead of the crowd.

Normally, when we make cake, we need milk and eggs, but during the Great Depression, people had to get creative because these ingredients were costly and hard to come by, so they created *wacky cake*. It's also a bit wacky because we make it right in the pan instead of a bowl! Today we're making Wacky But Wise Cake to remind us that following Jesus doesn't make sense to the world, but it's still the wise thing to do. We were created to change the world, not follow it.

WACKY BUT WISE CAKE

Ingredients

1 ½ cups all-purpose flour
1 cup granulated sugar
¼ cup unsweetened cocoa powder
1 tsp. baking soda
½ tsp. salt
2 tsp. vanilla extract
1 tbsp. white vinegar
⅓ cup vegetable oil
1 cup water
You can enjoy this cake plain, with whipped cream and berries, or include a can of your favorite frosting if you prefer.

Directions

Preheat oven to 350°F.

In an 8x8" pan, sift together flour, sugar, salt, baking soda, and cocoa.

Use a spoon to create three separate holes in the dry ingredients. Pour the oil into one, the vinegar into the second, and the vanilla into the third hole.

Pour the water over the whole thing and then use a fork to stir it together well.

Bake for 27-35 minutes, until a toothpick inserted into the center comes out with a few crumbs.

Allow cake to cool and then enjoy plain or top with your favorite frosting or whipped cream and fresh berries.

APPENDIX A:
GLOSSARY OF BAKING TERMS

Combine – Stir the ingredients together just until they are all mixed in.

Cut In – This generally refers to a way of incorporating butter and flour to create small sandy pieces when making pastries. If you don't have a pastry cutter, you cut small chunks of butter into the flour using two forks or butter knives like you were cutting apart meat.

Cream – Usually refers to beating together butter and sugar by adding air into the mixture to produce a light, fluffy texture. You'll typically start with this step when a recipe calls for butter and sugar. Then you add eggs one at a time to continue the creaming process.

Double Boiler – Filling a saucepan with a couple inches of water and heating it to boil, then placing another pan or heatproof bowl over top of the saucepan (should be big enough that it fits snugly and doesn't fall into the bottom saucepan, but shouldn't touch the water). This allows the heat from the boiling water on the bottom to steam the chocolate or other substance without burning it.

Dust – Lightly sprinkle a dry ingredient such as powdered sugar, cocoa, flour, etc.

Fold – Using a rubber spatula, gently combine two items by moving the spatula from the bottom of the bowl up and over the top of the mixture. Rotate the bowl and continue mixing until they are combined without deflating the mixture.

Grease – Use cooking spray, butter, or oil to lightly coat the inside of your baking pan to keep your dessert from sticking to it.

Knead – Using a dough hook on a stand mixer, or your hands, fold dough over and press down, then rotate it and continue to help it develop gluten strands that strengthen breads and doughs.

Lukewarm – refers to a temperature that is slightly warm, but not hot to the touch, typically around 105°F Fahrenheit.

Sift – Use a sieve over a bowl and place your powdered sugar, flour, etc. in the sieve then gently tap it against the palm of your hand to shake all the powder into the bowl. This prevents big clumps and makes the mixture smoother.

Soft Peaks – Whip egg whites or heavy cream to the point where the egg white or cream becomes light and fluffy so that if you pull the whisk out, you will see a point (peak) that bends over immediately.

Stiff Peaks – When whipping egg whites or heavy cream longer, you can pull your whisk straight up out of the mixture, and it has a solid peak that doesn't bend over.

Zest – Use a zester (or cheese grater) to grate off the outside of a citrus fruit (lime, lemon, orange) over a small bowl. Be sure to only scrape off the outer peel; the white underneath will be bitter. This zest gives a bright and fresh citrus flavor to your dessert.

APPENDIX B: LIST OF EMOTIONS

Abandoned

Affectionate

Afraid

Aggravated

Aggressive

Agreeable

Alarmed

Amazed

Amused

Angry

Annoyed

Anxious

Apprehensive

Ashamed

Astonished

Awed

Awkward

Baffled

Bashful

Bereaved

Bewildered

Bitter

Blissful

Bold

Bothered

Brave

Calm

Cantankerous

Capable

Carefree

Careful

Cautious

Charitable

Cheerful

Cold

Complacent

Composed

Compulsive

Concerned

Confident

Contemptuous

Content

Contrite

Cooperative

Cranky

Crushed

Curious

Daring

Defiant

Dejected

Depressed

Detached

Disappointed

Discouraged

Disengaged

Disillusioned

Dismayed

Dismissive

Distant

Eager

Ecstatic

Edgy

Elated

Embarrassed

Emboldened

Enraged

Enthusiastic

Envious

Euphoric

Excited

Exhausted

Fatigued

Fearful	Hurt	Loving	Obstinate
Flustered	Hysterical	Mad	Offended
Foolish	Ignorant	Manic	Optimistic
Forgiving	Impatient	Manipulated	Outraged
Frightened	Inadequate	Marvelous	Overjoyed
Frustrated	Indifferent	Mean	Overloaded
Fulfilled	Insecure	Meek	Overstimulated
Furious	Inspired	Melancholy	Panicked
Generous	Inquisitive	Mischievous	Peaceful
Glad	Interested	Miserable	Peeved
Gleeful	Irked	Misunderstood	Pensive
Gloomy	Irrational	Moody	Perturbed
Grateful	Irritated	Mopey	Petrified
Greedy	Isolated	Morose	Petty
Grief-stricken	Jaded	Naïve	Petulant
Grouchy	Jealous	Naughty	Playful
Grumpy	Jittery	Needed	Pleased
Guarded	Joyful	Needy	Powerful
Guilty	Judged	Neglected	Powerless
Happy	Judgmental	Neglectful	Preoccupied
Heartbroken	Keen	Nervous	Prideful
Helpless	Kind	Nice	Proud
Hesitant	Lackluster	Nonchalant	Puzzled
Hopeless	Lazy	Numb	Qualified
Horrified	Leery	Obedient	Quarrelsome
Humbled	Lethargic	Obligated	Quiet
Humiliated	Lonely	Obsessed	Quirky

Rational	Sociable	Unsteady	Youthful
Rattled	Sorrowful	Unsure	Zany
Reasonable	Spiteful	Uplifted	Zealous
Reassured	Startled	Useful	
Rebellious	Stressed	Useless	
Refreshed	Stubborn	Vain	
Rejuvenated	Sympathetic	Valued	
Relaxed	Tearful	Vexed	
Relieved	Temperamental	Vibrant	
Reluctant	Terrified.	Victimized	
Remorseful	Thankful	Victorious	
Resentful	Threatened	Violent	
Reserved	Timid	Vivacious	
Restless	Tired	Volatile	
Sad	Tolerant	Vulnerable	
Safe	Torn	Wary	
Sarcastic	Tranquil	Weak	
Satisfied	Troubled	Whiny	
Scared	Trusting	Willful	
Secure	Unafraid	Wistful	
Sensitive	Unappreciated	Withdrawn	
Serene	Uncertain	Witty	
Serious	Uncomfortable	Worn	
Silly	Undecided	Worried	
Sincere	Uneasy	Worthless	
Skeptical	Unhappy	Wronged	
Smug	Unnerved	Yearning	

ABOUT THE AUTHOR

Katie J. Trent is a licensed clinical social worker (LCSW), a respected leader in the Christian homeschool community, and the founder of Family Faith-Building Academy. She has over a decade of experience in counseling children, teens, and families, having served as clinical director of two mental health agencies and as an elementary school counselor before transitioning to homeschooling and writing.

Along with her husband James, Katie also has more than fifteen years of ministry and church planting experience. In addition to *Recipes for a Sweet Child*, she authored *Dishing Up Devotions: 36 Faith-Building Activities for Homeschooling Families*.

Through writing, blogging, and speaking, Katie loves to inspire women to grow their faith, strengthen their families, and simplify their homeschool journeys. She has been a featured speaker at many homeschool conferences and has written for the Upper Room, Crosswalk, *The Christian Journal* magazine, homeschooling and parenting blogs, and other ventures.

Katie received her B.A. in social work from Boise State University and her master's in social work from Northwest Nazarene University. She and James have a daughter and son, Kendra and Jordan.

Connect with Katie at KatieJTrent.com for more resources to help you put the fun back into the fundamentals of family discipleship.

More Family Faith-Building Resources

For more resources to grow your faith, strengthen your family, and simplify your homeschool, go to KatieJTrent.com. Katie shares information on giveaways, new resources, freebies, events, and product reviews.

Katie also invites you to join Family Faith-Building Academy, an eight-week digital course designed to equip Christian parents to effectively disciple their kids in fun, meaningful, and memorable ways. Enrollment for individuals opens several times a year; groups such as co-ops, moms' groups, and churches can sign up anytime at discounted rates.

Learn more at FamilyFaithBuildingAcademy.com.

Creative Character-Building

Katie's book *Dishing Up Devotions: 36 Faith-Building Activities for Homeschooling Families"* offers thirty-six weekly activities to help your family build biblical character in fun and meaningful ways. Learn more at DishingUpDevotions.com.

Help Other Families

If you enjoy this book, you can make a huge difference by leaving a review on Amazon, Goodreads, and other sites. Your quick review helps other families find this resource, and it's a nice way to express your appreciation to an author. It means a lot to Katie, so thank you in advance for your review.

Join the Fun

Katie loves to see pictures of families using and enjoying her resources. Please tag her @KatieJTrent and #BakingJesusFamous when sharing photos on social media so she can see and share the post.

Questions?

Katie is always happy to help other moms, particularly those who homeschool. Please email her anytime at Katie@KatieJTrent.com.